CH00645862

A N

A C T

(Passed 9th January, 1799,)

To repeal the Duties imposed by an Act, made in
the last Session of Parliament, *for granting an Aid
and Contribution for the Prosecution of the War*;

AND

TO MAKE MORE EFFECTUAL PROVISION FOR THE LIKE PURPOSE,

BY GRANTING CERTAIN

DUTIES upon INCOME,

IN LIEU OF THE SAID DUTIES.

LONDON:

Printed by GEORGE EYRE and ANDREW STRAHAN,
Printers to the King's most Excellent Majesty.

1799.

This scarce antiquarian book is included in our special *Legacy Reprint Series*. In the interest of creating a more extensive selection of rare historical book reprints, we have chosen to reproduce this title even though it may possibly have occasional imperfections such as missing and blurred pages, missing text, poor pictures, markings, dark backgrounds and other reproduction issues beyond our control. Because this work is culturally important, we have made it available as a part of our commitment to protecting, preserving and promoting the world's literature. Thank you for your understanding.

ANNO TRICESIMO NONO

GEORGII III. Regis.

C A P. XIII.

An Act to repeal the Duties imposed by an Act, made in the last Session of Parliament, for granting an Aid and Contribution for the Prosecution of the War; and to make more effectual Provision for the like Purpose, by granting certain Duties upon Income, in lieu of the said Duties. [9th January 1799.]

Moft Gracious Sovereign,

WE, Your Majefty's moft dutiful Preambl and loyal Subjects, the Commons of *Great Britain* in Parliament affembled, being defirous to raife an ample Contribution for the Profecution of the War; and taking Notice that the Provifions made for that Purpofe, by an Act of the laft Seffion of Parliament, intituled, *An Act for* 38 *Geo.* 1 *granting to His Majefty an Aid and Contribu-* c. 16, ret *tion for the Profecution of the War*, have in fundry Inftances been greatly evaded, and

A 2 that

that many Perfons are not affeffed under the
faid Act in a juft Proportion to their Means
of contributing to the Publick Service; have
cheerfully and voluntarily given and granted,
and do by this Act give and grant, unto
Your Majefty, the feveral and refpective
Rates and Duties herein-after mentioned:
And we do moft humbly befeech Your Majefty that it may be enacted; and be it enacted by the King's moft Excellent Majefty,
by and with the Advice and Confent of the
Lords Spiritual and Temporal, and Commons, in this prefent Parliament affembled,

So much thereof as im-
pofes addi-
tional Duties,
or appoints
Commiffion-
ers, repealed;
from *April* 5,
1799;

and by the Authority of the fame, That fo
much of the faid recited Act, as charges any
Perfon with an additional Duty, in Proportion to the Amount of the Rates or Duties,
to which fuch Perfon was or fhould be affeffed according to any Affeffment or Affeffments made in purfuance of any Act or Acts
in force at the Time of paffing the faid recited Act, or as authorizes or appoints Commiffioners for executing the fame, or for
hearing and determining Appeals, fhall be,
and the fame is hereby repealed from and
after the Fifth Day of *April* One thoufand

except in cer-
tain Particu-
lars.
[*See* § 8, 9.]

feven hundred and ninety-nine: Save and
except in Cafes herein-after mentioned; and
in all Cafes relating to the recovering, collecting, paying, or accounting for any Arrears of the Rates or Affeffments charged by
virtue of the faid Act, which may become
payable on or before the faid Fifth Day of
April One thoufand feven hundred and ninety-nine,

ty-nine, and may after that Time remain unpaid; or to the recovering any Penalty or Forfeiture which fhall have been then incurred under and by virtue of the faid Act.

II. And be it further enacted, That, inftead of the Rates and Affeffments by the faid Act impofed and hereby repealed as aforefaid, and during the Term herein-after mentioned, there fhall be raifed, levied, collected, and paid annually, unto and for the Ufe of His Majefty, His Heirs and Succeffors, throughout the Kingdom of *Great Britain,* upon all Income arifing from Property in *Great Britain* belonging to any of His Majefty's Subjects, although not refident in *Great Britain*; and upon all Income of every Perfon refiding in *Great Britain,* and of every Body Politick or Corporate, or Company, Fraternity, or Society of Perfons (whether Corporate or not Corporate) in *Great Britain*; whether any fuch Income as aforefaid fhall arife from Lands, Tenements, or Hereditaments, wherefoever the fame fhall be fituate, in *Great Britain* or elfewhere, or from any Kind of perfonal Property, or other Property whatever, or from any Profeffion, Office, Stipend, Penfion, Employment, Trade, or Vocation, the feveral Rates and Duties following, (that is to fay); One One-hundred-and-twentieth Part of the Income of every fuch Perfon, Body Politick or Corporate, Company, Fraternity, or Society, eftimated according to this Act, if the

The following new Duties fhall be impofed on all Income, from Property in *Great Britain,* belonging to Subjects tho' not refiding there; and upon all Income of all Perfons refiding, and of all Corporations, etc. in *Great Britain,* whether arifing from Lands in *Great Britain* or elfewhere; or from Perfonal Property; or from any Profeffion, Office, Trade, etc. viz. From

6ol. to 6 s l. $\frac{1}{120}$th Part of fuch Income.

same shall amount unto Sixty Pounds *per Annum*, and shall be under Sixty-five Pounds

65*l.* and under 70*l.*; $\frac{1}{95}$ *per Annum*: One Ninety-fifth Part of such Income, if the same shall amount to Sixty-five Pounds, but shall be under Seventy

70*l.*—75*l.*; - $\frac{1}{70}$ Pounds: One Seventieth Part of such Income, if the same shall amount to Seventy Pounds, but shall be under Seventy-five

75*l.*—80*l.*; - $\frac{1}{65}$ Pounds: One Sixty-fifth Part of such Income, if the same shall amount to Seventy-five Pounds, but shall be under Eighty

80*l.*—85*l.*; - $\frac{1}{60}$ Pounds: One Sixtieth Part of such Income, if the same shall amount to Eighty Pounds, but shall be under Eighty-five Pounds: One

85*l.*—90*l.*; - $\frac{1}{55}$ but shall be under Eighty-five Pounds: One Fifty-fifth Part of such Income, if the same shall amount to Eighty-five Pounds, but

90*l.*—95*l.*; - $\frac{1}{50}$ shall be under Ninety Pounds: One Fiftieth Part of such Income, if the same shall amount to Ninety Pounds, but shall be under Nine-

95*l.*—100*l.*; $\frac{1}{45}$ ty-five Pounds: One Forty-fifth Part of such Income, if the same shall amount to Ninety-five Pounds, but shall be under One

100*l.*—105*l.*; $\frac{1}{40}$ hundred Pounds: One Fortieth Part of such Income, if the same shall amount to One hundred Pounds, but shall be under One

105*l.*—110*l.*; $\frac{1}{38}$ hundred and five Pounds: One Thirty-eighth Part of such Income, if the same shall amount to One hundred and five Pounds, but shall be under One hundred and ten

110*l.*—115*l.*; $\frac{1}{36}$ Pounds: One Thirty-sixth Part of such Income, if the same shall amount to One hundred and ten Pounds, but shall be under One hundred and fifteen Pounds:

115*l.*—120*l.*; $\frac{1}{34}$ One Thirty-fourth Part of such Income, if
the

the fame fhall amount to One hundred and fifteen Pounds, but fhall be under One hundred and twenty Pounds: One Thirty-fecond Part of fuch Income, if the fame fhall amount to One hundred and twenty Pounds, but fhall be under One hundred and twenty-five Pounds: One Thirtieth Part of fuch Income, if the fame fhall amount to One hundred and twenty-five Pounds, but fhall be under One hundred and thirty Pounds: One Twenty-eighth Part of fuch Income, if the fame fhall amount to One hundred and thirty Pounds, but fhall be under One hundred and thirty-five Pounds: One Twenty-fixth Part of fuch Income, if the fame fhall amount to One hundred and thirty-five Pounds, but fhall be under One hundred and forty Pounds: One Twenty-fourth Part of fuch Income, if the fame fhall amount to One hundred and forty Pounds, but fhall be under One hundred and forty-five Pounds: One Twenty-fecond Part of fuch Income, if the fame fhall amount to One hundred and forty-five Pounds, but fhall be under One hundred and fifty Pounds: One Twentieth Part of fuch Income, if the fame fhall amount to One hundred and fifty Pounds, but fhall be under One hundred and fifty-five Pounds: One Nineteenth Part of fuch Income, if the fame fhall amount to One hundred and fifty-five Pounds, but fhall be under One hundred and fixty Pounds: One Eighteenth Part of fuch Income, if the fame fhall amount to One hundred and fixty

Marginal notes:

120l. and under 125l. $\frac{1}{32}$

125l.—130l.; $\frac{1}{30}$

130l.—135l.; $\frac{1}{28}$

135l.—140l.; $\frac{1}{26}$

140l.—145l.; $\frac{1}{24}$

145l.—150l.; $\frac{1}{22}$

150l.—155l.; $\frac{1}{20}$

155l.—160l.; $\frac{1}{19}$

160l.—165l.; $\frac{1}{18}$

A 4   Pounds,

Pounds, but shall be under One hundred
and sixty-five Pounds: One Seventeenth
Part of such Income, if the same shall amount
to One hundred and sixty-five Pounds, but
shall be under One hundred and seventy
Pounds: One Sixteenth Part of such Income, if the same shall amount to One hundred and seventy Pounds, but shall be under
One hundred and seventy-five Pounds: One
Fifteenth Part of such Income, if the same
shall amount to One hundred and seventy-
five Pounds, but shall be under One hundred and eighty Pounds: One Fourteenth
Part of such Income, if the same shall amount
to One hundred and eighty Pounds, but
shall be under One hundred and eighty-five
Pounds: One Thirteenth Part of such Income, if the same shall amount to One hundred and eighty-five Pounds, but shall be
under One hundred and ninety Pounds:
One Twelfth Part of such Income, if the
same shall amount to One hundred and
ninety Pounds, but shall be under One hundred and ninety-five Pounds: One Eleventh
Part of such Income, if the same shall amount
to One hundred and ninety-five Pounds, but
shall be under Two hundred Pounds: And
One Tenth Part of such Income, if the same
shall amount to Two hundred Pounds, or
upwards: Which respective Rates shall be
charged and assessed by Commissioners, to be
chosen for that Purpose in the Manner herein-after directed.

III. And

Marginal notes:

165*l.* and under 170*l.* $\frac{1}{17}$

170*l.*—175*l.*; $\frac{1}{16}$

175*l.*—180*l.*; $\frac{1}{15}$

180*l.*—185*l.*; $\frac{1}{14}$

185*l.*—190*l.*; $\frac{1}{13}$

190*l.*—195*l.*; $\frac{1}{12}$

195*l.*—200*l.*; $\frac{1}{11}$

200*l.* or upwards $\frac{1}{10}$

III. And be it further enacted, That every Person having a Child or Children born in Wedlock, and maintained principally by such Person at his or her Expence, whether such Child or Children be the Child or Children of him or her, or of his or her Wife or Husband by any former Marriage, shall be entitled to the respective Abatements following, (that is to say); Any Person whose Income is Sixty Pounds a Year or upwards, and under Four hundred Pounds a Year, having such Child or Children, shall have an Abatement after the Rate of Five Pounds *per Centum* for each such Child : Any Person whose Income is Four hundred Pounds a Year or upwards, and under One thousand Pounds a Year, an Abatement after the Rate of Four Pounds *per Centum* for each such Child, where any of the Children are or is of an Age exceeding Six Years ; and where all such Children are under the Age of Six Years, then an Abatement after the Rate of Three Pounds *per Centum* for each such Child : Any Person having an Income of One thousand Pounds a Year or upwards, and under Five thousand Pounds a Year, an Abatement after the Rate of Three Pounds *per Centum* for each such Child, where any of such Children are or is of an Age exceeding Six Years ; and where all such Children are under that Age, then an Abatement after the Rate of Two Pounds *per Centum* for each such Child : And all Persons having an Income of Five thousand Pounds a Year or upwards,

upwards, an Abatement after the Rate of
Two Pounds *per Centum* for each such Child,
where any of such Children are or is of an
Age exceeding Six Years; and where all
such Children are under the Age of Six
Years, then an Abatement after the Rate of
One Pound *per Centum* for each such Child :
Which Abatements shall be allowed by the
respective Commissioners for the Purposes of
this Act, and for hearing and determining
Appeals under this Act, upon Delivery of a
Declaration stating the Number of such
Person's Children, and on Proof made, to
the Satisfaction of the said Commissioners,
of the Truth of the Matters contained in
such Declaration ; and the said Commissioners shall cause the said Abatements to be deducted from the Amount of such Person's
Assessment, as the Case shall require.

This Act not to affect the Stock of Friendly Societies established under 33 *Geo.* III, c. 54.

IV. Provided always, and be it further
enacted, That nothing in this Act contained
shall be construed to extend to charge the
Stock or Fund of any Friendly Society established under or by virtue of an Act, passed
in the Thirty-third Year of the Reign of His
present Majesty, intituled, *An Act for the En-
couragement and Relief of Friendly Societies.*

Nor Corporations, &c. established for charitable Purposes only.

V. Provided also, and be it further en-
acted, That no Corporation, Fraternity, or
Society of Persons established for charitable
Purposes only, shall be chargeable under this
Act, in respect of the Income of such Cor-
poration, Fraternity, or Society.

VI. Pro-

VI. Provided alfo, and be it further en- Nor :
acted, That no Annual Officer prefiding n'ual i
over any Corporation or Royal Burgh, fhall Corpc
be chargeable by virtue of this Act in re- for h
fpect of the Income derived from his Salary cial I
and Emoluments in refpect of fuch Office.

VII. Provided alfo, and be it further en- Recto
acted, That no Rector or Vicar fhall be not c
charged in refpect of any Stipend paid to a Curat
Curate, fuch Rector or Vicar being ufually ries.
refident, and ordinarily doing Duty in fome
Parifh of which he is Rector or Vicar, or
having fome other legal Excufe for not refiding on fuch Rectory or Vicarage.

VIII. Provided alfo, and be it further en- Perfo
acted, That no Perfon who fhall, on or after fiding
the paffing of this Act, actually be in *Great* in Gr
Britain for fome temporary Purpofe only, tain,
and not with any View or Intent of eftablifh- unde
ing his or her Refidence therein, fhall be Act, l
chargeable with the Duties impofed by this c. 16.
Act as a Perfon actually refiding in *Great
Britain*, but fhall be chargeable neverthelefs
with any Duties to which fuch Perfon might,
on or after the faid Fifth Day of *April* One
thoufand feven hundred and ninety-nine, be
chargeable by virtue of the faid Act of the
Thirty-eighth Year of His Majefty's Reign,
if this Act had not been made; and the
faid Act of the Thirty-eighth Year of His
Majefty's Reign, and all the Provifions
therein contained, fhall be in full Force,
with

with refpect to fuch Perfon, as if this Act had not been made.

If the Income of fuch Perfons be charged under that Act and this, Deduction may be made on Account of fuch double Charge.

IX. Provided alfo, and be it further enacted, That if the Income of any Perfon, being in *Great Britain* for fuch temporary Purpofe only, or any Part thereof, fhall be charged under the faid recited Act, and alfo under this Act, it fhall be lawful for the refpective Commiffioners for the Purpofes of this Act, or for hearing and determining Appeals under this Act, on Proof upon Oath of a double Charge, to make fuch Deduction on Account thereof, as to the faid refpective Commiffioners fhall feem juft and proper.

Perfons occafionally abfent from *Great Britain*, at the Time of the Execution of this Act, fhall be charged under this Act on the Whole of their Income.
[*See* § 38, 39, 73, 88.]

X. And be it further enacted, That any Subject of His Majefty, whofe ordinary Refidence fhall have been in *Great Britain*, and who fhall have departed from *Great Britain*, and gone into any Parts beyond the Seas, for the Purpofe only of occafional Refidence, at the Time of the Execution of this Act, fhall be deemed, notwithftanding fuch temporary Abfence, a Perfon chargeable in refpect of his or her Income, as a Perfon actually refiding in *Great Britain*; and fhall be affeffed and charged accordingly (in the Manner herein-after directed) upon the whole Amount of his or her Income, whether the fame fhall arife from Property in *Great Britain* or elfewhere, or from any Profeffion,

Profeffion, Office, Penfion, Stipend, Employment, Trade, or Vocation, in *Great Britain* or elfewhere.

XI. And be it further enacted, That the refpective Perfons authorized or appointed to be Commiffioners for executing, and acting in the Execution of, the Acts relative to the Duties on Houfes, Windows, or Lights, or other the Duties placed under the Management of the Commiffioners for the Affairs of Taxes, fhall, from Time to Time, caufe Lifts to be made of fuch Perfons who are or fhall be named or defcribed in or by any Act or Acts paffed or to be paffed in the prefent or any future Parliament, to act as Commiffioners of Land Tax or Supply, or other the Duties aforefaid, within their County, Riding, Shire, Stewartry, or Place, and who fhall be qualified as by this Act is required, and Ten other Perfons at the leaft, alfo fo qualified, for each Divifion of fuch County or Riding, and for each City, Borough, Town, or Place in *England,* for which Commiffioners are or fhall be feparately named in fuch Act or Acts, or for each Shire, Stewartry, or Place in *Scotland,* if fo many Perfons can be found qualified as by this Act is required, or fo many as can be found fo qualified therein refpectively; for which Purpofe the faid acting Commiffioners, or any Two of them, acting for any Divifion of any County or Riding, or any City, Borough, Town, or Place in *England,*

I

The a&
Commi
ers of 1
Houfe 7
&c. fha
Lifts to
made o
Commi
ers of I
Tax, &
their C
&c. qu
as direc
this Ac
§ 23.]
others
lified i
Divifio
if fo m
be four
fhall ap
Day fo
Firft N
for fuc
pofe, v
Days i
being i
ed by i
fpector
and fh
ver fui
figned
them,
Clerk,
tranfn
the Ti
fice; v
caufe
be laic
Perfor
ing, v
Years
ing, fe

been returned on the Pannel to ferve) as Grand Jurors for each County, &c. in *England*; (at a Meeting to be fummoned by the Sheriff within 10 Days after Receipt of fuch Lifts;) and before the Barons of the Exchequer in *Scotland.* Such Grand Jurors and Barons fhall felect a competent Number, duly qualified, from fuch Lifts, to be Commiffioners under this Act; and for fupplying Vacancies, in the Order in which they fhall be felected: If a fufficient Number cannot be found qualified, the Deficiency may be fupplied from the Lifts of the adjoining Counties, &c. The Number of Commiffioners in any One Diftrict not to exceed

England, or for any Shire, Stewartry, or Place in *Scotland,* who fhall receive Notice of this Act, fhall appoint a Day and Time for holding the Firft Meeting for the Purpofe of making out fuch Lifts as aforefaid, (containing the Places of Refidence refpectively of the Perfons named therein to act within their refpective Divifions, Cities, Boroughs, Towns, or Places, in *England,* and Shires, Stewartries, and Places in *Scotland*); which Meeting fhall be holden within the Space of Seven Days after any Two Commiffioners of fuch Divifion, City, Borough, Town, or Place in *England,* or Shire, Stewartry, or Place in *Scotland,* fhall be required by any Infpector or Surveyor to hold the fame: And the faid Commiffioners prefent at any Meeting held for the Purpofes aforefaid, fhall make out and deliver fuch Lifts, figned by the Majority of the Commiffioners prefent at fuch Meeting, to the Clerk of fuch Commiffioners, who fhall forthwith tranfmit the fame to the Commiffioners for the Affairs of Taxes; who fhall (in refpect of Lifts made in *England*) caufe the fame to be laid before fuch Perfons who fhall have ferved, or have been returned upon the Pannel of Jurors to ferve, as Jurors upon the Grand Inqueft of the County at large, or of the City, Borough, Town, or Place, being refpectively a County of itfelf, at any Affize or Seffions of Oyer and Terminer and General Gaol Delivery, within the Space of Four Years before the paffing of this Act; or fo

many

many of them as fhall be prefent at any Meeting to be holden in purfuance of the Summons of the Sheriff for the fame County, City, Borough, Town, or Place, (which Summonfes the faid Sheriffs, or their Deputies refpectively, fhall caufe to be iffued, returnable within Ten Days after the Tranfmiffion of fuch Lifts to them refpectively); and in refpect of Lifts made in *Scotland*, the fame fhall be laid before the Barons of the Exchequer there: And the Perfons prefent at fuch Meeting, and the faid Barons refpectively fhall, out of fuch Lifts, felect fuch Number of Perfons, qualified as hereby is required, as fhall be neceffary for carrying into Execution the general Purpofes of this Act, and for fupplying from Time to Time any Vacancy that may arife as hereinafter mentioned; and fhall appoint fuch Perfons to be Commiffioners for fuch Purpofes, in and for the whole County, Riding, Shire, Stewartry, City, Borough, Town, or Place, in the Order in which they fhall be felected to ferve; and if in *England* fhall appoint who and what Number fhall act for each Divifion of any County or Riding, and for each City, Borough, Town, or Place therein, for which Commiffioners are or fhall be feparately named as aforefaid: And if the Perfons prefent at the faid Meeting, or the faid Barons refpectively, fhall not find in any Lifts fufficient Numbers of Perfons qualified to be Commiffioners, they fhall felect fuch Number from the

Lifts

Five, nor
lefs than T
and their
Names to I
returned t
the Tax C
fice.

Lifts of any adjoining or neighbouring Division or Divifions of the fame County, Riding, or Place, or from the County at large adjoining to any City, Borough, or Town, being a County of itfelf, if in *England*; and if in *Scotland*, from the Lifts of any adjoining or neighbouring Shire, Stewartry, or Place, as may be neceffary: And fuch Perfons fhall be declared to be fo appointed Commiffioners as aforefaid in the Order in which they fhall be felected and fet down in Writing by the faid Perfons and Barons refpectively, or the Majority of them there prefent; and they fhall be Commiffioners for the Purpofes of this Act in the Order in which they fhall be fo appointed: Provided always, That the Number of Commiffioners to be appointed to act together in any one Divifion, or in any City, Borough, Town, or Place in *England*, or any one Shire, Stewartry, or Place in *Scotland*, fhall not exceed the Number of Five, or be lefs than Two: And the Names of the Perfons fo to be appointed fhall from Time to Time be returned to the Commiffioners for the Affairs of Taxes at their Office.

Commiffion-
ers not re-
ftrained from
acting in any
other Part of
the County,
etc.

XII. Provided always, and be it further enacted, That nothing herein contained fhall be conftrued to reftrain the faid Commiffioners, or any of them, from acting as Commiffioners in any other Part of the County, Riding, or Place, for which they are appointed.

XIII, And

XIII. And be it further enacted, That any Persons, qualified as by this Act is required, may at any Time after such Lists shall be returned, cause their Names to be inserted in such Lists, by giving Notice thereof to the Commissioners for the Affairs of Taxes.

XIV. And be it further enacted, That the several Clerks of Assize shall, as soon as conveniently may be after the passing of this Act, transmit to the Commissioners for the Affairs of Taxes, true and perfect Copies of the several Pannels of Persons returned within the Period before mentioned, to serve as Jurors as aforesaid, within the several and respective Counties, Ridings, Cities, Towns, and Places in *England*, who are empowered by this Act to select and appoint Commissioners under this Act; and the proper Officers in *Scotland* shall, in like Manner, return to the said Barons Lists of Persons who shall have been summoned to serve as Jurors in *Scotland*, within the like Period; which Lists, together with the Lists of Persons qualified to act as Commissioners under this Act, the said Commissioners for the Affairs of Taxes shall transmit to the said Sheriffs, with Directions to them to summon, within the Time herein-before limited, the respective Persons who are empowered as aforesaid to select and nominate Commissioners at such Places as such Sheriffs shall respectively name; which Summons shall respectively be

B   by

by publick Advertisements, signed by such Sheriffs or their Deputies, and inserted in some Newspapers usually circulated in the respective Counties, Ridings, Shires, Stewartries, and Places aforesaid, Four Days at least before the Day to be named for the Meeting of such Persons for the Purposes before mentioned.

In *Lincolnshire* Lists shall be returned by Commissioners for the Hundreds and Subdivisions in *Lindsey*, &c. and separate Commissioners be chosen for such Hundreds, &c.

XV. Provided also, and be it further enacted, That, within the County of *Lincoln*, Lists of Persons, qualified to act as Commissioners for the Purposes of this Act, shall be returned by the respective Commissioners acting for the several Hundreds and Subdivisions within the several Divisions of *Lindsey*, *Holland*, and *Kesteven*, within the said County; and that separate Commissioners shall be chosen to act within those respective Hundreds and Subdivisions, in like Manner as herein-before directed to be done, within the several Divisions of the other Counties herein mentioned.

The said Grand Jurors, &c. shall appoint Three Persons qualified as directed in § 23 to be Commissioners of Appeal in each County, and three more to supply Vacancies,

XVI. And be it further enacted, That the said Persons who shall have served, or have been returned to serve on the Grand Inquest as aforesaid, in *England*, and the Barons of the Exchequer in *Scotland*, shall appoint Three Persons, qualified as herein directed, to act as Commissioners of Appeal for each County at large, Riding, Shire, or Stewartry in *Great Britain*, and also Three other Persons at the least, if so many can be found

found qualified, in like Manner to supply Vacancies as herein is mentioned : And the Names of such Persons shall be returned to the Commissioners for the Affairs of Taxes at their Office; who shall give Notice of such Appointment to such Commissioners of Appeal; who shall forthwith appoint a Time and Place for their First Meeting, for the Purpose of hearing and determining Appeals to be made by virtue of this Act, which shall be Ten Days at least before the First Instalment of the Duty granted by virtue of this Act shall become payable : And such Meeting or Meetings shall be held from Time to Time, with or without Adjournment, so long as any such Appeal shall be depending : And the said Commissioners of Appeal shall also, Ten Days at the least before any subsequent Instalment of the Rates hereby granted shall become payable, in case any Appeals shall be then depending, hold a Meeting or Meetings at such Time or Times and Place as shall be appointed by them, for hearing and determining such Appeals; and that such Meetings shall from Time to Time be held, with or without Adjournment, so long as any such Appeal shall be depending : And the said Commissioners of Appeal shall cause publick Notice to be given of their said First and subsequent Meetings for the Purpose of hearing and determining Appeals, in the Manner herein directed.

B 2   XVII. Pro-

Marginal note: whose Names shall be returned to Tax Office who shall them Notice of their Appointment on which Commissioners shall appoint their Meeting for hearing Appeals at least Ten Days before the first Instalment becomes due and subsequent Meetings Ten Days before every Instalment, if necessary, and give Notice thereof; such Meetings to be held from Time to Time till all Appeals are heard.

In *London* the Mayor, Aldermen, and Common Council shall elect Six qualified persons; (Three of whom shall be Aldermen;) from which Number the Mayor and Aldermen shall choose Three; the Bank shall also choose Two other Persons; the *East India* Company, the *South Sea* Company, and the *Royal Exchange* and *London* Insurance Companies, each One; to be Commissioners for *London*.

XVII. Provided always, and be it further enacted, That within and for the City of *London*, the Mayor, Aldermen, and Common Council, in Common Council assembled, shall elect Six Persons, qualified as herein is required, Three of whom at the least shall be Aldermen; out of which Number so to be elected the Mayor and Aldermen shall choose Three: And the Governors and Directors of the Bank of *England* shall choose Two other Persons: And the Directors of the United Company of Merchants of *England* trading to the *East Indies*, shall choose One other Person: The Sub-Governor, Deputy Governor, and Directors of the *South Sea* Company, shall choose One other Person: And the Governors and Directors of the *Royal Exchange* Insurance Company, and the Governors and Directors of the *London Insurance* Company, shall each choose One other Person, qualified as by this Act is required: And the Three Persons so chosen by the Mayor and Aldermen, together with the other Persons respectively chosen as aforesaid, shall be Commissioners for the Purposes of this Act, within and for the said City of *London*: And the Names of the Persons so chosen shall be returned to the Commissioners for the Affairs of Taxes.

The Three Commissioners of Appeal in *London* shall be chosen, One by the

XVIII. And be it further enacted, That within and for the said City of *London*, the Commissioners for hearing and determining Appeals shall be chosen as follows; *videlicet,*
the

the said Mayor and Aldermen of the said City shall choose One Person to be such Commissioner: The said Governors and Directors of the Bank of *England*, the said Directors of the United *East India* Company, and the said Governors and Directors of the *South Sea* Company, shall choose One other Person to be such Commissioner: And the said respective Governors and Directors of the several Insurance Companies before-mentioned, shall choose a Third Person to be such Commissioner: And the Three Persons so chosen as last aforesaid, shall be Commissioners for hearing and determining Appeals within and for the said City: And their Names shall be returned to the Commissioners for the Affairs of Taxes.

Mayor Alderm One by Bank, India C pany, a South Se pany; One by Two In rance C nies.

XIX. Provided always, and be it further enacted, That within and for the County of *Middlesex*, (except the District of the *Tower Hamlets*, called *The Tower Division*), the Sheriff shall cause to be summoned such Jurors only who shall have been returned from the Hundred of *Ossulston*, in the said County, on the Pannel of the Grand Jury in the Court of our Lord the King before the King Himself at *Westminster*, within the Period before mentioned.

For Mid. (excep: Tower D vision) t Sheriff s summon Grand J only as a returned the Pann Westminst Hall.

XX. And be it further enacted, That within and for the District of the *Tower Hamlets*, commonly called *The Tower Division*, in the County of *Middlesex*, it shall be lawful for

For the Division, Lieutena &c. of t Tower f summon

acting Justices, who shall select Commissioners and Assistants to the Commercial Commissioners for such Division.

[See § 98, 110, &c.]

When a Commissioner, or Commissioner of Appeal, shall die or decline to act, the Person next in Order in the Lists shall be appointed in his Room; and the Grand Jurors, &c. shall from Time to Time select and add

for the Lieutenant of the Tower of *London*, or Deputy Lieutenant, or Major thereof, to summon the Justices of the Peace acting in and for the said Division at the Time of passing this Act, and who shall continue so to act until they shall be so respectively summoned: And such Justices being so summoned shall select the several and respective Commissioners to act for such Division under this Act for any of the Purposes herein mentioned, in the same Manner, and with the same Powers, as the Grand Inquest of any County is hereby empowered to do, and also certain other Persons to supply Vacancies as they shall arise, in the Manner before-mentioned; and also so many other Persons as they shall think necessary, to be Assistants to the Commercial Commissioners to be appointed under this Act: And the Names of the Persons so chosen shall be returned to the Commissioners for the Affairs of Taxes.

XXI. And be it further enacted, That when and so often as any One or more of the Commissioners for the Purposes of this Act, or any of the Commissioners for hearing and determining Appeals under this Act, named or appointed to act for any County, Riding, Shire, Stewartry, or Place in *Great Britain*, or any Division, City, Borough, Town, or Place within the same, shall die, or decline to act in the Execution of the Powers and Trusts thereof, or, having begun to act, shall decline to act any further therein, then

then and in every such Case, the Person or Persons, next in Order on such Lists, shall be appointed the Commissioner or Commissioners, in the Place of the Commissioner or Commissioners so refusing or declining to act, or dying: And the Jurors who shall from Time to Time serve on the Grand Inquest at the Assizes or Sessions of Oyer and Terminer and General Gaol Delivery, and the several and respective Persons beforementioned, in *England*, and the Barons of the Exchequer in *Scotland*, shall respectively, as often as Occasion shall require, select and add new Names to the Persons before selected; who shall respectively in their Order be a Commissioner or Commissioners for the Purposes of this Act, or a Commissioner or Commissioners of Appeals, as the Case may require, as and when any such Vacancy shall happen: And when any such Commissioner appointed to act for any City, Borough, Town, or Place shall die, or refuse or decline to act as aforesaid, then and in every such Case, the Place of the Commissioner so dying, or refusing or declining to act, shall be filled up in such Manner, and by the same Persons, as the said Commissioner was appointed.

XXII. And be it further enacted, That every Person to be appointed a Commissioner for the Purposes of this Act, and every Person appointed to hear and determine Appeals, before he shall begin to act therein

B 4 (except

(except in adminiſtering the Oath herein-
after expreſſed) ſhall take the following
Oath; (that is to ſay),

Oath,

'I *A. B.* do ſwear, That I will truly, faith-
'fully, impartially, and honeſtly, ac-
'cording to the beſt of my Skill and Know-
'ledge, execute the ſeveral Powers and Au-
'thorities veſted in me by an Act of the
'Thirty-ninth Year of the Reign of His
'Majeſty King *George* the Third, intituled,
'[*Here ſet forth the Title of this Act*]: And
'that I will exerciſe the Powers entruſted
'to me by the ſaid Act, in ſuch Manner
'only as ſhall appear to be neceſſary for the
'due Execution of the ſame: And that I
'will judge and determine upon all Matters
'and Things which ſhall be brought before
'me under the ſaid Act, without Favour,
'Affection, or Malice: And that I will not
'diſcloſe any Particular contained in any
'Schedule of Income, or any Evidence or
'Anſwer given by any Perſon who ſhall be
'examined or make Affidavit reſpecting the
'ſame, except in ſuch Caſes and to ſuch
'Perſons only where it ſhall be neceſſary to
'diſcloſe the ſame for the Purpoſes of this
'Act, or in order to, or in the Courſe of, a
'Proſecution for Perjury committed in ſuch
'Examination or Affidavit.

'So help me GOD.'

to be admini-
ſtered by any
Commiſſion-

Which Oath any One of the reſpective Commiſſioners appointed for the Purpoſes of this
Act,

Act, or to hear and determine Appeals under the same, is hereby authorized to administer; and which Oath so taken shall be subscribed by the Party taking the same; and the Names of all Persons so subscribing shall, within One Month afterwards, be transmitted to the Office of the Commissioners for the Affairs of Taxes: And if any Person shall act as a Commissioner for the Purposes of this Act, or as a Commissioner for hearing and determining Appeals, before he shall have taken the Oath herein mentioned (except in administering the same), he shall, for every such Offence, forfeit and pay the Sum of One hundred Pounds, to be recovered as any Penalty may be recovered by the said first recited Act.

er, and subscribed by Party swearing, and the Names returned to the Tax Office

Penalty on acting as a Commissioner, without taking the Oath, 100l.

XXIII. Provided always, and be it further enacted, That no Person shall be capable of acting as a Commissioner for the Purposes of this Act, within or for any County at large, Riding, Shire, Stewartry, City, Borough, Town, or Place in *Great Britain,* who shall not be possessed of a Personal Estate of the Value of Ten thousand Pounds; or who shall not be seised or possessed of an Estate of the like Nature, and of Thrice the Value or more, as is or shall be required as the Qualification of a Commissioner to act in the Execution of an Act, passed in the Thirty-eighth Year of the Reign of His present Majesty, intituled, *An Act for granting an Aid to His Majesty by a Land Tax, to*
be

Qualification of Commissioners for Counties at large, &c. 10,000l. Personal Estate, or Thrice the Value of the Qualification required for a Commissioner of Land Tax.

be raised in Great Britain, *for the Service of
the Year One thousand seven hundred and ninety-
eight,* in such County at large, Riding,
Shire, Stewartry, City, Borough, Town, or
Place; or shall be the Heir Apparent of a Person seised or possessed of an Estate of the like
Nature, and of Thrice the Value, or more,
of the Estate of which a Person ought to be
seised or possessed in order to qualify his Heir
Apparent to be a Commissioner to act in the

No Commis-
sioner shall be
capable of
being a Com-
missioner of
Appeals.

Execution of the said Act: Nor shall any
Person be capable of acting as a Commissioner for hearing and determining Appeals in
pursuance of this Act, in any County, Riding,
Shire, or Stewartry, who shall be a Commis-

Qualification
of Commis-
sioners of Ap-
peal to be
Twice the
Value of that
required for
Commission-
ers.

sioner for the Purposes of this Act; nor unless
such Person shall in like Manner be possessed
of a Personal Estate of the Value of Twenty
thousand Pounds; or be seised or possessed of
an Estate of the like Nature, and of Twice
the Value, or more, as is required by this
Act, for a Commissioner for the Purposes of
this Act as aforesaid; or shall be Heir Apparent of some Person who shall in like
Manner be seised or possessed of a like Estate
as aforesaid, of Twice the Value, or more,
of the Estate of which a Person ought to be
seised or possessed in order to qualify his
Heir Apparent to be a Commissioner for the
Purposes of this Act.

Qualification
of Commis-
sioners in
Cities (being

XXIV. Provided also, and be it further
enacted, That no Person shall be capable of
acting as a Commissioner for the Purposes
of

of this Act, within or for any City, Borough, Town, or Place, being respectively a County of itself, who shall not be possessed of a Personal Estate of the Value of Three thousand Pounds; or be seised or possessed of an Estate of the like Nature and of Three Fifths of the Value, as is required by this Act for a Commissioner for the Purposes of this Act, within a County at large: Nor within any of the Inns of Court, Inns of Chancery, or Liberty of the Rolls, who shall not be possessed of a Personal Estate of the Value of Three thousand Pounds, or be seised or possessed of an Estate of the like Nature and Value as is required by this Act for a Commissioner for the Purposes of this Act for any Borough, Town, or Place: And that within and for any such City, Town, or Place, being a County of itself, the Magistrates and Justices of the said City, Town, or Place, shall be summoned, together with such Jurors as aforesaid, to act in the Selection and Nomination of the respective Commissioners to be appointed under this Act.

XXV. Provided also, and be it further enacted, That nothing herein contained shall be construed to require more than One Third of any Qualification, consisting of Lands, Tenements, or Hereditaments, to be situate within the respective County, Riding, Shire, or Stewartry, for which any Person shall be appointed to act as a Commissioner.

XXVI. Pro-

Land and
Personalty
may be valued
together as a
Qualification:
100*l.* Personalty to be
equivalent to
4*l. per Annum*
from Land.

XXVI. Provided alfo, and be it further
enacted, That any Perfon whofe Eftate fhall
confift of Lands, Tenements, or Hereditaments, and alfo of Perfonal Eftate, to any of
the refpective Values herein-before required,
eftimating in every fuch Cafe One hundred
Pounds Perfonal Eftate, and Four Pounds
per Annum of Eftate in Lands, Tenements,
or Hereditaments, as equivalent to each
other, may act as a Commiffioner for any of
the Purpofes of this Act, as if fuch required
Value had wholly arifen from Lands, Tenements, or Hereditaments, or wholly from
Perfonal Eftate; any Thing in this Act contained to the contrary notwithftanding.

Penalty on a
Commiffioner
acting without
being fo qua-
lified 50*l.*

[§ 114.]

XXVII. And be it further enacted, That
if any Commiffioner for any of the Purpofes
of this Act before or after mentioned, or any
other Perfon herein required to be feifed or
poffeffed of a Qualification to act in the Execution of this Act, fhall act therein, or in
any of the Powers therein contained and
vefted in fuch Commiffioner, or other Perfon
as aforefaid, without being duly qualified as
by this Act is required, every fuch Perfon
fhall forfeit and pay, for every fuch Offence,
the Sum of Fifty Pounds; to be recovered
as any Penalty may be recovered by virtue
of the faid firft recited Act.

If there be not
a fufficient
Number of
Commiffion-

XXVIII. Provided alfo, and be it further
enacted, That in cafe there fhall not be a
fufficient Number of Commiffioners for the
Purpofes

Purposes of this Act, for any City, Borough, Town, or Place, for which by this Act such Commissioners are particularly to be appointed, capable of acting according to the Qualification required by this Act, then in every such Case any of the Commissioners for the Purposes of this Act, appointed for the County at large within which such City, Borough, Town, or Place shall be situate, or next adjoining thereto, may and they are hereby required to act as Commissioners for the Purposes of this Act, for such City, Borough, Town, or Place.

ers duly qualified for any City, etc. Commissioners for the County at large may act within such City, etc.

XXIX. Provided also, and be it further enacted, That if there shall not have been a grand Inquest impannelled within the Period before-mentioned, in any City, Town, or Place, being a County of itself, it shall be lawful for the Sheriff of such City, Town, or Place, to summon the Persons named in the Commission of the Peace for such City, Town, or Place, at the Time of passing this Act, and who shall continue so to act until they shall be so respectively summoned; and such Magistrates and Justices, being so summoned, shall select the several and respective Commissioners to act for such City, Town, or Place, under this Act, for any of the Purposes herein-mentioned, in the same Manner, and with the same Powers, as the Grand Inquest of such City, Town, or Place, if impannelled within the Period before-mentioned, together with such Persons in the

If no Grand Jury shall have been impannelled in any City, etc. within the Time mentioned in § 11, the Sheriff may summon the acting Justices of the Peace for such City, etc. who shall then select the Commissioners for the same.

Commission

Commiſſion of the Peace, might have done; and alſo certain other Perſons to ſupply Vacancies, as the ſame ſhall ariſe, in the Manner before-mentioned; and alſo ſo many other Perſons as they ſhall think neceſſary to be Aſſiſtants to the Commercial Commiſſioners to be appointed under this Act, if any ſhall be appointed for ſuch City, Town, or Place: And the Names of the Perſons ſo choſen ſhall be returned to the Commiſſioners for the Affairs of Taxes.

If it ſhall appear that One Set of Commiſſioners of Appeal cannot perform the Duty for the whole County or Riding, Two or more Sets may be named to act for ſeveral Diviſions; and then a Commiſſioner of Appeal may be a Commiſſioner under this Act in another Diviſion.

XXX. Provided always, and be it further enacted, That if it ſhall appear to the Perſons aſſembled for the Purpoſe of naming Commiſſioners of Appeals as aforeſaid for any, County or Riding in *England*, that by Reaſon of the Extent of ſuch County or Riding, or the relative Situations of different Parts thereof, one Set of Commiſſioners of Appeal cannot conveniently perform the Duties required of ſuch Commiſſioners by this Act, it ſhall be lawful for ſuch Perſons to name Two or more Sets of Commiſſioners of Appeal to act for different Parts of ſuch County, or Diviſions of ſuch County or Riding, deſcribing, in an Order to be made by ſuch Perſons for ſuch Purpoſe, for what Part of ſuch County or Riding, each of ſuch Sets of Commiſſioners of Appeal ſhall reſpectively act; and in ſuch Caſes it ſhall be lawful for any Perſon acting as a Commiſſioner of Appeal for one Part of ſuch County or Riding, to act as a Commiſſioner for the Purpoſes

Purpofes of this Act in any other Part of
fuch County or Riding, in which he fhall
have no Jurifdiction as a Commiffioner of
Appeal.

XXXI. And be it further enacted, That
it fhall be lawful for the Commiffioners for
the Purpofes of this Act, and alfo for the
Commiffioners appointed for hearing and determining Appeals under this Act, and they
are hereby refpectively authorized and empowered, in any Matter before them concerning the Execution of this Act, to examine any Perfon or Perfons willing to be
examined in fuch Matter, and to adminifter
an Oath or folemn Affirmation to fuch Perfon or Perfons, according to the Directions
of this Act, and alfo to receive any Affidavit
or Depofition in Writing upon Oath or Affirmation, which fhall be made in fuch Manner as by the faid firft recited Act of the
Thirty-eighth Year before-mentioned is required with refpect to Affidavits or Depofi-
tions taken under the Authority of that Act,
and alfo any Affidavit or Depofition in
Writing upon Oath or Affirmation, which
fhall be made in any Parts beyond the Seas,
before any Magiftrate of the Country, Ter-
ritory, or Place, where the Perfon making
fuch Oath or Affirmation fhall alfo refide,
and which fhall be certified and tranfmitted
to the faid refpective Commiffioners under
the Hand and Seal of fuch Magiftrate; provided that in every Affidavit, Depofition,

*Commiffion-
ers and Com-
miffioners of
Appeal may
examine on
Oath any
Perfons wil-
ling to be ex-
amined, and
may receive
Affidavits
and Depofi-
tions in Writ-
ing, in any
Matter before
them con-
cerning the
Execution of
this Act.*

*Requifites in
fuch Affida-
vits, &c.*

or

or Affirmation, there be expreffed the Addition of the Party making the fame, and the particular Place of his or her Abode, and the fame be entitled an Affidavit, Depofition, or Affirmation, made in purfuance of this Act.

Perfons giving falfe Evidence on fuch Examination, &c. fhall be liable to the Penalties of Perjury. XXXII. And be it further enacted, That if any Perfon upon any fuch Examination on Oath or Affirmation, or in any fuch Affidavit, Depofition, or Affirmation, fhall wilfully and corruptly give falfe Evidence, or fhall wilfully and corruptly fwear or affirm any Matter or Thing which fhall be falfe or untrue, every fuch Perfon fo offending, and being thereof duly convicted, fhall be and is hereby declared to be fubject and liable to fuch Pains and Penalties as by any Law now in being Perfons convicted of wilful and corrupt Perjury are fubject and liable to.

Indictments, etc. may be tried in the County where the Affidavit, &c. was exhibited. XXXIII. And be it further enacted, That any Indictment or Information for Perjury committed in any fuch Affidavit, Depofition, or Affirmation, as aforefaid, whether the fame fhall be taken or made within *Great Britain* or without, fhall and may be laid, tried, and determined, in the County where fuch Affidavit, Depofition, or Affirmation, fhall be exhibited to the Commiffioners, in purfuance of this Act.

Surveyors and Infpectors to take the following XXXIV. And be it further enacted, That the feveral Surveyors and Infpectors, who are åre or shall be appointed to put in Execution this present Act, shall, before they shall respectively enter upon their Office, take the following Oath; (that is to say),

' I A. B. do swear, That in the Execution Oath.
'   of an Act, intituled, [*here set forth the*
' *Title of this Act*], I will examine and revise
' all Statements delivered within my District;
' and in surcharging the Schedules of In-
' come, and in objecting to Deductions made
' therefrom, I will act according to the best
' of my Information and Knowledge: And
' that I will conduct myself therein without
' Favour, Affection, or Malice: And that I
' will exercise the Powers entrusted to me by
' the said Act, in such Manner only as shall
' appear to me to be necessary for the due
' Execution of the same, or as I shall be
' directed by the Commissioners for the Af-
' fairs of Taxes, or any Three or more of
' them: And that I will not disclose any Par-
' ticular contained in any Statement or Sche-
' dule of Income, or any Evidence or An-
' swer given by any Person who shall be
' examined or make Affidavit, Deposition,
' or Affirmation, respecting the same in pur-
' suance of the said Act, except in such
' Cases, and to such Persons only, where it
' shall be necessary to disclose the same for
' the Purposes of the said Act, or in order
' to, or in the Course of, a Prosecution for
' Perjury committed in such Examination or
' Affidavit.   ·   ' So help me GOD.'

C   XXXV. And

Clerk to the refpective Commiffioners to take the following

XXXV. And be it further enacted, That every Perfon to be appointed a Clerk to the faid refpective Commiffioners fhall, before he fhall enter upon his Office, take the following Oath; (that is to fay),

Oath.

' I *A. B.* do fwear, That I will not difclofe
' any Particular contained in any State-
' ment or Schedule of Income, or any Evi-
' dence or Anfwer given by any Perfon who
' fhall be examined or make Affidavit, De-
' pofition, or Affirmation, refpecting the
' fame, in purfuance of an Act, intituled,
' [*here fet forth the Title of this Act,*] except
' in fuch Cafes, and to fuch Perfons only,
' where it fhall be neceffary to difclofe the
' fame for the Purpofes of the faid Act, and
' as I fhall be directed fo to do by Two at
' leaft of the Commiffioners acting for the
' Divifion or Place for which I have been
' appointed, or in order to, or in the Courfe
' of, a Profecution for Perjury committed
' in fuch Affidavit, Depofition, or Affir-
' mation.

' So help me GOD.'

Powers, &c. of 38 *Geo.* III, c. 16, and all other Acts relative to the Duties under the Management of the Commiffioners of Taxes, extended to

XXXVI. And be it further enacted, That the feveral Commiffioners who fhall be appointed for the Purpofes of this Act, and alfo the feveral Perfons appointed, or to be appointed Infpectors, Surveyors, Affeffors, or Collectors, to put in Execution the faid Act, paffed in the Thirty-eighth Year of the Reign of His prefent Majefty, intituled, *An*
Act

Act for granting to His Majesty an Aid and Contribution for the Prosecution of the War, or the several Acts relative to the Duties this Act; except where expresly varied by this Act. under the Management of the Commissioners for the Affairs of Taxes, or any of them, shall, and they are hereby respectively empowered and required to do all Things neceflary for putting this Act in Execution, with relation to the Rates and Duties hereby granted, in the like, and in as full and ample a Manner, as they or any of them are or is authorized to put in Execution the Acts above-mentioned, or any of them, or any Matters or Things therein contained : And the Rates and Duties hereby granted shall and may be ascertained, managed, collected, recovered, paid over, and accounted for, under such Penalties, Forfeitures, and Disabilities, and according to such Rules, Methods, Directions, and Provisions as the Rates and Affessments granted by the said Act passed in the Thirty-eighth Year beforementioned, and other the Rates and Duties now under the Management of the Commissioners for the Affairs of Taxes, or any of them, are, or is, or may be ascertained, managed, collected, recovered, paid over, and accounted for, (except as far as any of the said Rules, Methods, Directions, and Provisions are expresly varied by this Act); and all and every the Powers, Authorities, Rules, Directions, Methods, Penalties, Forfeitures, Clauses, Matters, and Things contained in the said Act, or any Act of the

same

fame Seffion of Parliament relating thereto,
for the affeffing, furcharging, mitigating,
abating, vacating, hearing, determining, or
adjudging the Affeffments on the Amount
of the Rates to be charged under the Authority of the faid Act, or for advancing or paying the Rates and Duties charged thereby,
either to the Bank of *England*, or to the Collectors appointed for that Purpofe, or for
accounting for the fame; and alfo all the
Powers, Authorities, Rules, Penalties, Claufes, Matters, and Things, contained in any
Act or Acts relating to the Duties under the
Management of the Commiffioners for the
Affairs of Taxes, (as far as the fame feveral
Powers, Authorities, Rules, Directions,
Methods, Penalties, Forfeitures, Claufes,
Matters, and Things, are refpectively applicable to the Rates and Duties granted by this
Act, and not exprefsly varied or otherwife
provided for hereby), fhall feverally and refpectively be in full Force, and duly ob-
ferved, practifed, and put in Execution
throughout the Kingdom of *Great Britain*,
for the feveral Purpofes of this Act, as fully
and effectually, to all Intents and Purpofes,
as if the fame Powers, Authorities, Rules,
Directions, Methods, Penalties, Forfeitures,
Claufes, Matters, and Things, were particularly repeated and re-enacted in the Body of
this Act.

Commiffion-
ers acting
under the pre.

XXXVII. And be it further enacted,
That the Commiffioners acting in the Execution

cution of the Acts relative to the said present Duties shall, at their First Meeting to be held under this Act, as is herein-before directed, or any Two of them present at such Meeting, direct their Precept or Precepts to the Assessors of the several Parishes and Places within their respective Divisions, requiring them to appear before the said Commissioners at such Time and Place as they shall appoint, not exceeding Fourteen Days after such Precept; and shall, at such their Appearance, issue to such Assessors the Instructions and Directions duly filled up and signed by Two or more of them, and such Warrants under the Hands and Seals of Two or more of them, as the Surveyors and Inspectors shall have had delivered to them for that Purpose, under the Direction of the Commissioners for the Affairs of Taxes.

sent Acts shall, at their First Meeting, [see §11,] summon the Assessors to appear within 14 Days, and issue the Instructions and Warrants delivered by the Surveyors and Inspectors under Directions of the Tax Office. [See § 49.]

XXXVIII. And be it further enacted, That the Assessors of the Duties under the Management of the Commissioners for the Affairs of Taxes, for the Year ending on the Fifth Day of *April* One thousand seven hundred and ninety-nine, shall, within Fourteen Days after the Date of the Precept so to be delivered to them as aforesaid; and the Persons to be appointed Assessors of any of the Duties under the like Management, after the Fifth Day of *April* One thousand seven hundred and ninety-nine, shall, within Fourteen Days after the Date of the Precept which shall be issued to them by the Commissioners

Assessors shall yearly give Notice to Householders and Persons occupying distinct Apartments, to deliver within 14 Days Lists signed by them, containing the Name of every Lodger, Inmate, &c. (except Servants and Infants), resident in such House or Apartment;

C 3

and also Lists of Persons residing Abroad, Infants, married Women, &c. entitled to Income in the Receipt of such Householder as Trustee, and the Names of his Co-Trustees, if any ; and also of Persons receiving Income from Property of which any Householder is Trustee ; which Lists such Householder, etc. shall make out accordingly ; and also a Statement of the Sum he means to contribute, (according to a Form in Schedule B.) as not less than the just Proportion of his Income under this Act ; and also a like Statement of the Sum to be contributed by any Person whose Income such Householder, etc.

missioners for the Purposes of this Act, in every Year, during the Term herein mentioned, give Notice to every Householder within the Limits of the Places for which such Assessors shall so act, or leave the same at his or her Dwelling House: And, where any Dwelling House shall be let in different Apartments, and occupied distinctly by different Families or Persons, who shall either be separately and distinctly charged to the Duties on Windows and Lights, or where the Landlord of such Dwelling House shall, by reason of the same being so let, be charged to the said Duties, also give or leave the like Notice to or for the Occupier of each such distinct Apartment, to prepare and deliver, within Fourteen Days next ensuing the Day of serving such Notice, a List in Writing, containing, to the best of his or her Belief, the proper Name of each and every Lodger, Inmate, and other Person, (except Servants and Infants not having any Income chargeable by virtue of this Act), resident in such Dwelling House, or distinct Apartment ; and also a List, containing the proper Name of every Person not resident in *Great Britain,* and of every Infant, Idiot, Lunatick, and Married Woman, who shall have or be entitled to any Income chargeable by virtue of this Act, which shall be in the actual Receipt of such Householder or Occupier, as Trustee, Agent, Receiver, Guardian, Tutor, Curator, or Committee, or in any other Character, either separately,

or

or jointly with any other Person or Persons, and if jointly with any other Person or Persons, then the proper Name of every such other Person or Persons; and also the Name or Names of every other Person or Persons for whom any Householder or Occupier shall hold any Property as such Trustee, Guardian, Tutor, Curator, or Committee, the Income whereof shall be in the actual Receipt of such other Person or Persons: And every such Householder or Occupier shall, after such Notice so given or left, make out such Lists, and sign the same with his or her proper Name; and shall also at the same Time make out and deliver a Statement in Writing, signed by him or her, of the Sum which he or she means to pay under this Act, as his or her Contribution, (according to one of the Forms marked (B.) hereunto annexed, and as the Case may require), as being not less than the just Rate or Proportion of his or her Annual Income, estimated according to the Provisions of this Act, with which he or she ought to be charged by virtue thereof; and also a like Statement or Account in Writing, signed by him or her, of the Sum which he or she proposes should be contributed for and on Behalf of such other Person or Persons as aforesaid, for whom such Householder or Occupier is in the actual Receipt of any Income, as being not less than the just Rate and Proportion of the Annual Income of such other Person or Persons chargeable by virtue of this Act: Which

shall be in the actual Receipt of: Such Lists and Statements to be delivered to the Assessors within 14 Days: If the Householder, etc. neglect to deliver such Lists, etc. the Assessors shall return his Name and the Names of all such as ought to be returned by him in the Knowledge of the said Assessors. [See also, § 67]

Lifts and Statements, or such of them as the Case shall require, according to the Provisions of this Act, every such Householder or Occupier shall deliver or cause to be delivered to such Assessor or Assessors within the Space of Fourteen Days after Service of such Notice: And if any such Householder or Occupier shall refuse or neglect to make out and sign such Lifts or Statements, or either of them, as the Case may require, and deliver the same to the Assessor or Assessors within the Time before-mentioned, then such Assessor or Assessors shall return to the said Commissioners for executing this Act, the Names of any such Householders or Occupiers making such Default as aforesaid; and shall also make out a List, containing the Names of all such Lodgers, Inmates, and others, (except Servants and Infants not having any Income as aforesaid), resident in the Dwelling House of any such Householder or Occupier making such Default as aforesaid ; and also of all Persons for whom and on whose Behalf such Householder or Occupier ought to make out and deliver such Lift and Statement as aforesaid (if any such there be, within the Knowledge of such Assessor or Assessors).

On receiving Lifts of the Names of Lodgers, etc. Assessors shall give them Notice to return

XXXIX. And be it further enacted, That the said Assessors shall, within Seven Days after any such Lists of Lodgers, Inmates, and others, resident in any Dwelling House or distinct Apartment, shall be delivered to them

them as aforefaid, give or leave Notice in like Manner as aforefaid, to or for every Perfon fo returned to them as fuch Lodger or Inmate, or other Perfon refident as aforefaid, to make out and deliver, within Fourteen Days after the Day of ferving fuch Notice, the like Lift in Writing of the Perfons not refiding in *Great Britain*, and of Infants, Idiots, Lunaticks, and Married Women, who fhall have or be entitled to any Income chargeable by virtue of this Act, which fhall be in the Receipt of fuch Lodger or Inmate, or other Perfon refpectively, or fhall actually receive any Income derived from Property which fuch Lodger or Inmate fhall hold as fuch Truftee, Guardian, Tutor, Curator, or Committee, and of the Names of fuch other Perfons (if any) as fhall be joined with him or her as Truftee, Agent, or Receiver, Guardian, Tutor, Curator, or Committee, or in any other Character, as is hereby required to be made out and delivered by Houfeholders: And every fuch Lodger, Inmate, or other Perfon aforefaid, fhall make out fuch Lift, and deliver the fame figned as aforefaid; and fhall alfo make out and deliver fuch and the like Statements of the Sum he or fhe means to contribute on his or her own Account, and alfo propofes fhould be contributed for or on Behalf of any other Perfon or Perfons as aforefaid, as are hereby required to be made out and delivered by Houfeholders: Which Lifts or Statements, or fuch of them as the Cafe fhall require, according

cording to the Provisions of this Act as last mentioned, every such Person shall deliver to such Assessor or Assessors, within the Space of Fourteen Days after Service of such Notice: And if any such Person shall neglect or refuse to make out such Lists or Statements, or either of them, as the Case shall require, and deliver the same to the Assessor or Assessors within the Time before mentioned, then such Assessor or Assessors shall return to the Commissioners the Names of all such Persons making such Default as last aforesaid; and shall also make out a List containing the Names of all Persons of and for whom such Person making such Default ought to make out and deliver such Lists and Statements as aforesaid (if any such there be within the Knowledge of such Assessor or Assessors).

Act not to extend to Persons exempted by their Poverty from Poor Rates, &c.

XL. Provided always, and be it further enacted, That nothing herein contained shall be construed to require any Notice to be delivered to, or any List or Statement to be returned by, any Person residing in any Tenement whereof all the Inhabitants are, by Reason of their Poverty only, exempted from the actual Payment of the usual Rates and Taxes toward the Church and Poor.

Income of married Women shall be stated by their Husbands; but the Wife may be ex-

XLI. And be it further enacted, That the Income of any Married Woman, living with her Husband, shall be stated and accounted for by her Husband at the Time of delivering his own Statement under this Act; provided

provided that the Commiffioners fhall be at Liberty to fummon the Wife, and examine her touching her feparate Property, under fuch Rules and Regulations as any Party may by this Act be examined.

amined as to her feparate Property.

XLII. Provided always, and be it further enacted, That if any other Perfon, for whom fuch Perfon as aforefaid fhall act as Truftee, Agent, or Receiver, fhall be of full Age, and fhall refide in *Great Britain* at the Time required for the Return of fuch Lift as aforefaid, it fhall be fufficient for fuch Truftee, Agent, or Receiver, to return in fuch Lift the proper Name and Place of Refidence of fuch other Perfon, without making any Statement of the Sum to be contributed or paid for fuch other Perfon; which Lifts of other Perfons fo refident as aforefaid fhall be forthwith delivered to the Surveyor or Infpector where fuch Lift fhall be delivered, for the Information of the Commiffioners for the Affairs of Taxes.

If the cestui que Truft is of full Age and refides in Great Britain, it fhall be fufficient for the Truftee to return his Name and Refidence, to be delivered to the Surveyor, &.

XLIII. Provided alfo, and be it further enacted, That no Truftee who fhall have authorized the Receipt of the Income of any Truft Property, by or on the Behalf of the Perfon entitled thereto, and who fhall permit fuch Income to be received by the Perfon or Perfons fo authorized to receive the fame, fhall be deemed to be in the actual Receipt of fuch Income; but the Perfon or Perfons who fhall really and *bona fide* receive the

No Truftee who has authorized his cestui que Truft to receive the Income of Truft Property, nor any Banker, &c. of Perfons entitled to Income, fhall be deemed to be in the actual Receipt of fuch Income.

the fame for his, her, or their Ufe or Benefit under fuch Authority, fhall be deemed to be in the actual Receipt thereof within the Intent and Meaning of this Act: And that no Perfon who, as Banker, Agent, or Receiver, fhall receive any Income for the Ufe of any Perfon beneficially entitled thereto, and refident in *Great Britain*, fhall be deemed to be in the actual Receipt of fuch Income within the Intent and Meaning of this Act.

Affeffors fhall alfo yearly affix on the Church Doors, general Notices to all Refidents, to deliver their Lifts and Statements, which fhall be deemed good Notice to all fuch Refidents, though the Notice required in § 38, is not delivered to them.

XLIV. And be it further enacted, That the Affeffors appointed for the prefent Year ending as aforefaid, fhall, within Fourteen Days after the Date of fuch firft-mentioned Precept as aforefaid, and the Affeffors to be appointed for any fubfequent Year after the Fifth Day of *April* One thoufand feven hundred and ninety-nine, fhall, within Fourteen Days after the Date of fuch laft-mentioned Precept as aforefaid, in every Year during the Term herein mentioned, caufe general Notices to be affixed on the Doors of the Church or Chapel, and Market Houfe or Crofs (if any) of the City, Town, Parifh, or Place, for which fuch Affeffors fhall act, and if fuch Town or Place fhall not have a Church or Chapel, or Market Houfe or Crofs, then on the Church or Chapel Door of the next adjoining Parifh; requiring all Perfons refiding in the faid City, Town, Parifh, or Place, who are by this Act required fo to do, to make out and deliver to the refpective Affeffors fuch Lifts and Statements

ments as are hereby required; and such general Notice shall, from the Time when the same shall be affixed as aforesaid, be deemed sufficient Notice to all Persons resident in such City, Town, Parish, or Place, and the affixing the same in Manner before directed shall be deemed good Service of such Notice, notwithstanding such Notices as are herein-before directed shall not actually have been left at the House of any Householder, or at the Place of Residence of any Lodger or Inmate, or other Person resident within such Parish or Place: And the said respective Assessors shall cause the said Notices from Time to Time to be replaced (if necessary) for the Space of Ten Days before the Time required for the Delivery of such Lists and Statements as aforesaid: And every Person wilfully tearing, defacing, or obliterating any such Notice so affixed, during the said Space of Ten Days, shall forfeit, for every such Offence, a Sum not exceeding Twenty Pounds, to be recovered as any Penalty may be recovered under the said first recited Act, or this Act.

Persons defacing such Notices to forfeit not more than 20 l.

XLV. And be it further enacted, That the said Assessors shall, from Time to Time, within Three Days after the respective Times herein-before limited for the Delivery of the said Lists and Statements to them as aforesaid, (in case Commissioners shall be then appointed for the Purposes of this Act, or otherwise within Three Days after such Appointment),

Assessors shall regularly transmit to the Commissioners' Clerk, the Returns made to them, and Lists of the Names of Persons neglecting to make such Returns.

pointment), tranfmit to the Clerk to the faid Commiffioners for the Purpofes of this Act, in the Divifion or Place for which fuch Affeffors fhall act, all Returns then before made to the faid Affeffors, and alfo all Returns thereafter made to them within Three Days after their Receipt of the fame, to be laid before the faid Commiffioners at their Firft Meeting after their receiving the fame; and fhall alfo, as foon as conveniently may be, tranfmit to the faid Clerk Lifts of the Names of all Perfons who fhall have neglected to make any fuch Returns as aforefaid, to be laid before the faid Commiffioners at their Firft Meeting after the Receipt of fuch Lifts refpectively.

Affeffors fhall appear before Commiffioners at their Firft Meeting, and make Oath of the due Service of Notice on all Houfeholders, &c. and of affixing the general Notice; and to the Truth of the Statements of Lifts tranfmitted by them to the Commiffioners' Clerks.

XLVI. And be it further enacted, That every Affeffor fhall perfonally appear before the faid Commiffioners at their faid Firft Meeting, or fuch other Meetings as fuch Affeffor fhall be appointed to attend, and fhall make Oath or folemn Affirmation before them that the feveral Notices required to be delivered to Houfeholders and Occupiers, and alfo to Lodgers and Inmates, by this Act, have been duly ferved in the Manner required thereby upon all Houfeholders and Occupiers, and upon all Inmates and Lodgers, within the Limits of the Places for which fuch Affeffor fhall have been appointed, to the beft of his Knowledge: And that general Notices to the Effect mentioned in the faid Act have been duly affixed in the

8   Manner

Manner required by this Act on fuch proper Places within the City, Town, or Place, for which fuch Affeffor fhall act, as by this Act is required; and that the Statements delivered by him to the Clerk to the faid Commiffioners are all the Statements which have been returned to him in purfuance of this Act; and that the Lift delivered by him contains the Name of every Perfon within the faid Limits having made Default, or whofe Name ought to be returned according to the Directions of this Act, within the Knowledge of fuch Affeffor: And every Affeffor who fhall neglect to appear before fuch Commiffioners, and make fuch Oath or Affirmation, or who fhall not return any Statement of Income made to him, or fhall wilfully omit to return the Name or Names of any Perfon or Perfons who fhall not have returned any Statement or Lift, or whofe Name ought to be included in any Lift, as by this Act is required, fhall forfeit, for every fuch Offence, any Sum not exceeding Twenty Pounds, to be recovered as any Penalty may be recovered under the faid firft recited Act, or this Act.

Penalty on Neglect by Affeffor, in any Particular, not exceeding 20l.

XLVII. And be it further enacted, That if any Affeffor fhall, in the Execution of his Office under this Act, have conducted himfelf to the Satisfaction of the Commiffioners for the Purpofes of this Act, acting for the Divifion or Place where fuch Affeffor fhall be appointed, it fhall be lawful for the Commissioners

Commiffioners may certify to the Tax Office the good Conduct of the Affeffor, and what Reward they think due to him;

which the
Tax Office
may direct
the Receiver
General to
pay.

miffioners acting for fuch Divifion or Place, or the major Part of them prefent at any Meeting to be holden for that Purpofe, to grant to fuch Affeffor a Certificate of his good Conduct in fuch his Office; and fuch Commiffioners are thereupon required to report, in and by fuch Certificate, to the Commiffioners for the Affairs of Taxes, their Opinion as to the Sum which, in their Judgement, will be a fuitable Reward to fuch Affeffor for his Pains and Labour in fuch Office; Regard being had, in eftimating the Value of fuch Reward, to the Extent and Population of the Diftrict within which fuch Affeffor fhall have acted, and the Number of Perfons chargeable with the Rates and Duties granted by this Act, and his Diligence in the Execution of this Act: And it fhall be lawful for the Commiffioners for the Affairs of Taxes, upon fuch Certificate and Report, to grant fuch Reward to fuch Affeffor as to them fhall feem fit, not exceeding the Amount contained in fuch Certificate and Report, and to direct the Receiver General of the faid Rates and Duties to pay the fame to fuch Affeffor out of the Monies in his Hands arifing from the faid Rates and Duties.

Reward to
Surveyors, *etc.*
to be regu-
lated by Cer-
tificate of the
Commiffion-
ers.

XLVIII. Provided always, and be it further enacted, That no Reward fhall be given to any Surveyor or Infpector employed in the Execution of this Act, for his Service under the fame, unlefs the Commiffioners for executing this Act, or the Commiffioners for hearing and determining Appeals,

fhall

shall grant him a like Certificate of his good Conduct in such his Office, nor to any greater Amount than the said Commissioners granting such Certificate shall represent him to be entitled to.

XLIX. Provided always, and be it further enacted, That if the respective Commissioners of Land Tax and Supply, and other the present Duties before mentioned, shall omit to issue such Precepts to the respective Assessors in Manner before mentioned, it shall be lawful for any Justice of the Peace of the County, Riding, Shire, Stewartry, or Place, on Complaint of such Omission by any Surveyor or Inspector, to summon such Assessors before him, and upon their Appearance to issue to them the like Instructions, Directions, and Warrants, as the said Commissioners are hereby authorized to issue: And if any Assessor of the said Duties shall neglect to appear before the said Commissioners or Justice, according to the Directions of this Act, or to take upon himself the Execution of this Act, according to the Directions thereof, every such Assessor shall, for every such Offence, forfeit any Sum not exceeding Twenty Pounds, to be recovered as any Penalty may by the said first recited Act, or this Act, be recovered.

If Commissioners neglect to summon the Assessors, [see § 37.] the Justices of the County, etc. may do so, and give them their Instructions, etc.

Assessors refusing to appear before the Justice, to forfeit not exceeding 20l.

L. And be it further enacted, That the Commissioners acting in and for each Division shall, within Seven Days after the

The Commissioners shall, from Time to Time, make

D   Time

alphabetical Abſtracts in Books, of the Names, with the Contribution propoſed, *etc.* contained in the Liſts and Statements delivered; to which Books the Inſpectors ſhall have Acceſs, and may be furniſhed with Copies, *&c.*

Time fixed for the Delivery of ſuch Liſts or Statements, and ſo from Time to Time, cauſe an Abſtract of ſo many of the ſame as ſhall have been laid before them, containing the Names of all Perſons included in ſuch Returns as being chargeable by virtue of this Act, (arranged alphabetically), with their reſpective Places of Reſidence, and the Sums propoſed to be contributed, and alſo the Proportion which thoſe Sums bear to the Income aſſeſſed, to be prepared and entered in a Book or Books to be provided and kept by them; to which Book and Books every Inſpector and Surveyor, acting in the Execution of this Act, may have free Acceſs at all ſeaſonable Times, and ſhall, upon Demand, be furniſhed by the Clerk to the ſaid Commiſſioners with Copies thereof, or Extracts from the ſame, or ſuch Parts thereof as may be neceſſary for the due Execution of this Act.

The Commiſſioners ſhall appoint Meetings to take ſuch Statements into Conſideration, and compute and aſcertain the Aſſeſſments on ſuch Statements as they ſhall be ſatisfied with; and make Aſſeſſments accordingly.

LI. And be it further enacted, That the ſeveral and reſpective Commiſſioners for the Purpoſes of this Act ſhall appoint Meetings within their reſpective Diviſions, which ſhall be held not ſooner than Fourteen Days nor later than Twenty-one Days after ſuch Statements ſhall have been laid before them as aforeſaid, for the taking the ſame into Conſideration: And in caſe the ſaid Commiſſioners ſhall be ſatisfied that all or any of the ſaid Statements have been made truly and without Fraud, and ſo as to enable the Commiſſioners

missioners to charge the several Persons chargeable as aforesaid within their respective Districts, or any of them, with the full Duties with which they ought to be charged under this Act, or more; and in case no Information shall be given to the said Commissioners of the Insufficiency thereof, as herein-after is mentioned, the said Commissioners shall at such Meeting, or as soon after as conveniently may be, but not later than Seven Days after such Meeting, compute and ascertain, or cause to be computed and ascertained, the Amount of the Rates and Duties to be imposed upon such of the respective Persons chargeable by this Act, within their respective Districts, whose Statements shall be deemed satisfactory by such Commissioners, and shall make an Assessment upon each of those Persons accordingly.

LII. And be it further enacted, That in every Instance in which the said Commissioners shall not have received any Statement of the Income of any Person chargeable by virtue of this Act, or shall not have received any such Statement, with which they shall be satisfied; or if any Surveyor or Inspector for the said Rates and Duties shall apply to the said Commissioners for a Revision of any such Statement, suggesting in Writing that he hath Reason to believe that the Sum which would be chargeable on any Person upon such Statement, is less than the just Rate or Proportion of the Income of such Person, whereat

When the Commissioners have received no Statement, or no satisfactory one; or the Surveyor, etc. shall apply for the Revision of any Statement, suggesting its Deficiency in Writing, they shall issue a Precept to the Party chargeable who shall accordingly.

D 2

within 10 Days, return a Schedule of the Particulars of his Income; (according to Form D. in the Schedule.)

whereat he or she ought to be charged by virtue of this Act; or that any Person omitted in the Abstract, which shall be prepared by the said Commissioners, ought to be charged to the said Rates; the said Commissioners shall, unless they, or so many of them as are herein-after mentioned, after having heard such Reasons as the Surveyor shall lay before them, see Cause to disallow the Application of such Surveyor or Inspector, direct a Precept to such Person, in the Form marked (F.) in the Schedule annexed to this Act: Which Precept being delivered to or left at the last or usual Place of Abode of the Person chargeable as aforesaid, shall be binding upon such Person according to the Exigency of such Precept: And every such Person shall return or cause to be returned to the said Commissioners, within the Space of Ten Days after the Date of such Precept, a Schedule of the Particulars of Property from which the Income chargeable under this Act ought to be estimated, with the Amount of Deductions to be made therefrom under such of the Heads contained in and according to the Form marked (D.) in the Schedule annexed to this Act, as the Case shall require.

One Commissioner of less than Five present, or Two out of Five, may disallow the Application, &c. of

LIII. And be it further enacted, That unless all the Commissioners, except One, where less than Five shall be present, or all, except Two Commissioners where Five shall be present, shall adjudge that there is just Cause to disallow the Application of any Surveyor

veyor or Inspector to revise any Statement as aforesaid, it shall be lawful for the said Commissioners, and they are hereby required in every such Case, to disallow the same, and thereupon to compute and ascertain, or cause to be computed and ascertained, the Amount of the Rates and Duties which by this Act ought to be imposed upon the Person giving in such Statement in respect thereof, and to make an Assessment upon such Person accordingly, subject to such Appeal from the Determination of the said Commissioners, by such Surveyor or Inspector, as herein after is mentioned.

any Surveyor, etc. and the Commissioners shall then make the Assessment on the Party's own Statement as given in: (subject to Appeal under § 71).

LIV. And be it further enacted, That if any Person who shall have delivered any List, Statement, or Schedule, in pursuance of this Act, shall discover any Error therein, it shall be lawful for such Person to deliver a new or additional List, Statement, or Schedule, to the said Commissioners, in order to rectify such Error, and if such new or additional List, Statement, or Schedule, shall be so delivered before any Proceeding shall be had to recover any Penalty for not delivering the same, no Proceeding shall afterwards be had for recovering any such Penalty: And if any Proceeding shall have been actually had for recovering any such Penalty, it shall be lawful for the said Commissioners, upon Proof being made to their Satisfaction, that no Fraud or Evasion of this Act was intended, to certify the same under the Hands

Persons may correct Errors in their Lists or Statements by delivering a new List, etc. when no Proceeding shall be had for any Penalty incurred: Or if any such Proceeding be commenced, it may (on Certificate of Two Commissioners that no Fraud was intended) be stayed by the Court on a summary Application.

D 3   of

of any Two or more of them; and upon such Certificate, on Application in a summary Way to the Court where the same shall be commenced, all Proceedings for recovering such Penalty shall be stayed, either on Payment of the Costs of the Proceedings then had, if any, or without Payment of such Costs, as the said Court shall think fit and adjudge.

A Trustee shall not be liable to any Penalty for an imperfect Statement, if the Commissioners are satisfied that he was unable to deliver one more perfect; and if he deliver as perfect a Statement as he is able, from Time to Time, when required by the Commissioners.

LV. Provided always, and be it further enacted, That if any Trustee, Agent, or other Person hereby required to deliver any Statement or Schedule of any Income, of which such Trustee, Agent, or other Person shall be in the actual Receipt on Behalf of any other Person or Persons, shall deliver any Statement or Schedule which shall be imperfect, declaring himself, herself, or themselves to be unable to give a more perfect Statement or Schedule, with the Reasons for such Inability, such Person shall not be liable to any Penalty for not having delivered a Statement or Schedule, according to the Directions of this Act, in case the said Commissioners shall be satisfied that such Person was, at the Time of the Delivery of such Statement or Schedule, unable to deliver a more perfect Statement or Schedule, and in case such Person shall, upon the Requisition of the said Commissioners, deliver as perfect a Statement or Schedule as such Person shall from Time to Time be enabled to give.

LVI. Pro-

LVI. Provided always, and be it further enacted, That whenever the Time allowed by this Act for delivering any Statement or Schedule may not be sufficient for that Purpose, by reason of the Difficulty of ascertaining the Particulars or Amount of any Income or otherwise, it shall be lawful for the respective Commissioners, on Application to them for that Purpose, to enlarge the Time for delivering the same: And that no Person shall be liable to any Penalty for not having delivered such Statement or Schedule, for Delivery whereof such further Time shall be obtained, if the said Commissioners shall think fit so to order; and in such Case all Proceedings for Recovery of any such Penalty shall be staid, on a summary Application for that Purpose to the Court where such Proceeding shall be commenced: Provided always, That the said Commissioners shall not enlarge the Time for delivering such Statement beyond Forty Days, or the Time for delivering such Schedule beyond Thirty Days, before the Time when the First Instalment of the Duty, chargeable in respect of the Income to which such Statement or Schedule shall relate, would be payable if the same were duly charged with such Duty upon a Statement or Schedule delivered within the Time limited by this Act,

Commissioners may enlarge the Time for delivering in Statements and Schedules, to any Time not beyond 40 and 30 Days before the First Instalment of the Duty: Proceedings previously had for Penalties may be staid in a summary Way.

LVII. And be it further enacted, That the said Commissioners shall cause Assessments

Assessments shall be made (after 14 Days) by the

D 4

Commiffioners on fuch Schedules, which fhall be verified on Oath if required; but if no Schedule be returned, or an unfatisfactory one, and refufed to be verified on Oath, or if the Infpector, *etc.* has made any Surcharge, *etc.* on the fame, not difallowed by the Commiffioners; they fhall fummon the Party chargeable to attend, and be examined (on Three Days Notice), and alfo any other Perfons, to give them Information, and fhall examine them on all Points neceffary to afcertain the Charge to be made; but the Party fhall be at Liberty to amend his Schedule, before being required to verify it on Oath [*fee* § 59], and if the Commiffioners are fatisfi-

ments to be made and computed upon the Amount of Income contained in every fuch Schedule refpectively with which they fhall not be diffatisfied, as foon after the Expiration of Fourteen Days after fuch Schedule fhall be returned as they conveniently can, after calling upon the Party to verify the fame, upon Oath or Affirmation, if the faid Commiffioners fhall think the fame neceffary, in which Cafe fuch Oath or Affirmation fhall be final and conclufive: But if the faid Commiffioners fhall in any Inftance have received no fuch Schedule in purfuance of their Precept; or if they fhall not be fatisfied therewith, and the Party fhall not on the Requifition of the Commiffioners have verified fuch Schedule in Manner aforefaid; or if the Infpector or Surveyor fhall have made any Surcharge upon any fuch Schedule, or objected to any Deductions made thereupon, for the Purpofe of difcharging the fame, or any Part thereof, it fhall be lawful for the faid Commiffioners, and they are hereby required, unlefs they, or fo many of them as are herein-before mentioned, after having heard fuch Reafons as the Surveyor fhall lay before them, fee Caufe to difallow fuch Surcharge or Difcharge, in every fuch Cafe, to fummon the Party mentioned in any fuch Schedule, or in any fuch Notice or Certificate of Surcharge or Difcharge, before them to be examined, and alfo any other Perfon or Perfons whom they fhall think able to give Information refpecting the Income

come of fuch Perfon, at a Day and Place to be fixed by the faid Commiffioners, of which Three Days Notice at the leaft fhall be given to the Perfon or Perfons to be fummoned; and upon the Appearance of fuch Party fo to be charged before the faid Commiffioners, or any Two or more Commiffioners acting for the faid Divifion or Place, or upon the Appearance of any Perfon or Perfons fummoned to give Evidence, to receive and take Information, according to the Powers vefted in them by this Act, from the Party or other Perfons fo fummoned, and attending to give Evidence touching the Particulars mentioned in any fuch Schedule, or touching any other Particulars omitted to be mentioned, or of which no Schedule fhall have been delivered, and which ought to have been mentioned in fuch Schedule, or on fuch other Points as they fhall think neceffary to afcertain the Rate and Proportion with which fuch Perfon ought to be charged; provided that fuch Party fhall be at Liberty, at any Time before he or fhe fhall be called upon to verify his or her Schedule on Oath or folemn Affirmation, as herein-after is mentioned, to amend fuch Schedule in all fuch Particulars wherein he or fhe fhall fee Occafion ; and if the faid Commiffioners fhall not be diffatisfied with fuch amended Schedule, then an Affeffment fhall be made and the Rates and Duties computed thereupon in the Manner before directed.

ed with fuch amended Schedule, they may affefs the Party accordingly.

LVIII. And

All the Parties so summoned, (except the Party chargeable, or his confidential Agent), shall give their Evidence on Oath.

LVIII. And be it further enacted, That every Person who shall appear before the said Commissioners for the Purposes of this Act, in pursuance of such Summons as aforesaid, for the Purpose of giving any Testimony or Evidence touching or concerning any Rate or Assessment made or any Statement or Schedule delivered in pursuance of this Act, or touching any Doubt, Question, or Difficulty which shall arise relating thereto, (other than the Party to be charged and mentioned in such Schedule, or the Clerk, Agent, or Servant of, or other Person confidentially entrusted or employed in the Affairs of the said Party), shall, before he, she, or they shall proceed to give such Testimony or Evidence, take an Oath, or being One of the People called *Quakers*, a solemn Affirmation (which Oath or Affirmation any One or more of the said Commissioners is and are hereby authorized and required to administer) that the Testimony or Evidence to be given by him, her, or them, shall contain the whole Truth, and nothing but the Truth, in respect of the Matter or Question concerning which such Testimony or Evidence is to be given.

Where the Party chargeable, or his Agent attends, the Substance of their Evidence shall be reduced into Writing,

LIX. And be it further enacted, That where the Party mentioned in such Schedule, or the Clerk, Agent, or Servant of the Party or other Person confidentially entrusted or employed as aforesaid, shall appear before the said Commissioners for the Purpose of giving such Testimony or Evidence, then and

and in every such Case the Substance of the Testimony or Evidence given by any such last mentioned Person or Persons shall be, and the said Commissioners are hereby required to cause the same to be reduced into Writing, and to be read to the Person or Persons having given such Testimony or Evidence, before he, she, or they shall be called upon to verify the same according to the Directions of this Act; provided that in case he, she, or they shall, after such Testimony or Evidence shall be reduced into Writing, and read over to him, her, or them, be satisfied with the Substance of the Matter so reduced into Writing, he, she, or they shall swear or solemnly affirm to the Truth of the Substance thereof, (which Oath or Affirmation the said Commissioners, or any One or more of them, is and are hereby authorized to administer): Provided always, That any Person who shall appear to give any such Testimony or Evidence as last mentioned, shall be permitted to alter or amend any Part of his or her Testimony or Evidence, if he or she shall think proper, before he or she shall be called upon to verify the same: Provided also, That no such last mentioned Person shall be compelled to answer any Question which may be put to him or her by the said Commissioners for the Purposes of this Act, or any other Person or Persons whomsoever, before the said Commissioners in pursuance of this Act; but that every such last mentioned Person may decline peremptorily to answer any Question when-

ever

[sidenote:] and read to them, and they shall then swear to the Truth thereof; but they shall be first permitted to amend any Part of it; and shall not be compelled to answer any Question, but may decline peremptorily so to do.

ever he or she shall think proper, without shewing or alledging any Excuse for his or her so doing.

Surveyors, etc. having taken the Oath in § 34, may examine Lists of Householders, etc returned under the Act, and amend the same; and may also inspect and take Copies of the Statements returned; and may also examine and surcharge Schedules of Income returned to the Commissioners before the Partieschargeable are examined thereon; and may object to any improper Deductions therein; which Surcharges, etc. shall be considered by the Commifsioners, on Examination of the Parties; but Notice must be given by the Surveyor, to the Party charged, of the

LX. And be it further enacted, That it shall be lawful for the several Surveyors and Inspectors of the present Duties placed under the Management of the Commissioners for the Affairs of Taxes, and for any other Persons who shall be appointed to act as Surveyors and Inspectors in the Execution of this Act, who shall respectively have taken the Oath before stated, so as to bind him or them- not to disclose Particulars or Evidence as aforesaid, to inspect and examine all Lists of Householders, Lodgers, and, others, which shall be returned in pursuance of this Act, and to supply any Omissions which such Surveyor or Inspector may discover therein; and also to inspect and examine the several Statements which shall have been delivered in pursuance of this Act; and to take such Copies of, and Extracts from, the same, as they shall think requisite: And further, That it shall be lawful for such Surveyors and Inspectors to inspect and examine any Schedule of Income returned to the said Commissioners, before such Time as the Parties respectively, or Witnesses, shall have been examined before the said Commissioners touching the Truth thereof, and to surcharge the same according to the best of their Knowledge or Information; and to object to any Deductions, or any Part thereof, for the Purpose of discharging the same, which, in

the

the Judgement of the said Surveyors or Inspectors, ought not to be contained in such Schedule: Which Surcharges and Discharges respectively the said Commissioners shall take into their Consideration at the Time of such Examination of the Parties or Witnesses; provided that Notice in Writing shall have been given by such Surveyors or Inspectors to the Party to be charged, containing the particular Article or Articles mentioned in such Schedule, to which such Surveyor or Inspector shall object: And also it shall be lawful for the said Surveyors and Inspectors to inspect and examine any Rate or Assessment which shall be made under the Authority of this Act; and in case he or they shall find, at any Time before the said Commissioners shall have signed and allowed any Assessments, any Error in the same, or any of them, which in the Judgement of the said Surveyors and Inspectors shall require Amendment, it shall be lawful for the said Commissioners, and they are hereby required, upon sufficient Cause being shewn to them, to amend the same accordingly: And in case any Error shall be discovered in any Assessment after the same shall be allowed, it shall be lawful for the said Surveyors or Inspectors, and he or they is or are hereby required to certify the same to the said respective Commissioners, who shall have Power to cause the same to be amended, if in their Judgement they deem any Amendment requisite: Provided always, That Notice shall be given to

Marginal note: particular Objections to the Schedule: Surveyors, *etc.* may also inspect the Assessments previous to their being allowed by the Commissioners, in order to their being amended, and after Allowance the Assessments may also be amended on Certificate from the Surveyors *etc.* to the Commissioners: Notice of Amendment of Assessments shall be given to the Party affected, and to the Commissioners of Appeals, who shall appoint Times for hearing Appeals thereon; but no Appeal shall retard the Collection of the Rate; which shall be re amended where necessary by the Commissioners, after such Appeals are determined, so that the proper Rate shall be paid within the Year.

to the Party of any Amendment made in such Assessment by reason of such Surcharges or Discharges, in order that he may appeal from the same; and the respective Commissioners for hearing and determining Appeals shall also have Notice thereof, who are hereby respectively required, upon such Notice, to appoint, from Time to Time, in Manner herein-before directed, Days for hearing all Appeals made for any of the Causes last-mentioned, in such Manner and at such Times, within the Periods before limited, as shall be convenient: Provided also, That no Appeal from any Assessment to be made by virtue of this Act, shall retard the Execution of this Act so far as relates to the levying the Rates and Duties contained in such Assessment; but that it shall be lawful for the respective Officers employed in the Collection of the respective Rates or Duties hereby imposed, to cause the same to be levied in the mean Time, and until such Appeals shall be determined, as if no such Appeals had been made: Provided always, That after the Determination of such Appeals, the said respective Commissioners for the Purposes of this Act, shall cause the Assessments so appealed against to be amended according to such Determination, and the subsequent Payments to be adjusted thereby, so that the full Sums settled by the said Commissioners for hearing and determining Appeals, and no more, shall be paid within the Year.

LXI. Pro-

LXI. Provided alfo, and be it further enacted, That if upon the Determination of any fuch Appeals, it fhall appear to the faid Commiffioners that the Payments already made upon any fuch Affeffment, or any Part thereof, fhould be repaid, as being more than the full Sum which the Party affeffed ought to pay within the Year, or that the Party ought not to have been charged therewith under this Act, it fhall be lawful for the faid Commiffioners to rectify the Affeffments as the Cafes fhall refpectively require, and thereupon to grant Certificates thereof, ftating therein refpectively the Amount of the Sums to be repaid; and upon the Production of any fuch Certificate to the Receiver General of the County, Riding, or Place, where the fame fhall have been granted, or to his Deputy, if in *England*, or to the Receiver General of *Scotland*, the faid Receiver General refpectively fhall caufe the Amount contained in fuch Certificate to be paid out of any Monies in his Hands of the Rates and Duties hereby granted.

Where the Payments made exceed the Affeffment for One Year on a Certificate from the Commiffioners of Appeals, the Receiver General fhall repay the Overplus to the Party.

LXII. And be it further enacted, That it fhall be lawful for the faid refpective Surveyors and Infpectors, being fworn as aforefaid, to examine and infpect any Parochial Rates or Affeffments, fo far as relates to the Amount or Rate at which any Perfon may be affeffed therein; and alfo any Lift, or Pannel of Jurors, or Perfons fit to ferve on Juries, in the Cuftody of any publick Officer

Such Surveyors, etc. may examine Parifh Rates, and Lifts of Jurors; and, by Authority from Three Commiffioners of the Tax Office, may require from the proper Officer of

Corporations, Copies of Accounts relative to the Income of Members receiving Dividends from their Stock.

cer or Officers; and also for any Inspector or Surveyor, having Authority for that Purpose under the Hands of Three or more of the Commissioners for the Affairs of Taxes, to require from the proper Officer having in his Custody any Accounts of a publick Nature belonging to or kept by any Corporation or Company, a Copy of such Part or Parts thereof as may relate to the Income of any Person or Persons, or any Member or Members of such Corporation or Company, who shall have received any Dividends or Interest from the Funds or Stock of such Corporation or Company, or shall be entitled to the same.

After Examination of any Party chargeable, or in case of his Non-appearance or Refusal to be examined, the Commissioners shall ascertain his Rates, and make an Assessment on him; and send Copies of the same to the Collectors and to the Commissioners of Appeal; and shall issue Warrants to the Collectors, who shall give Notice of the Amount of

LXIII. And be it further enacted, That after such Examination taken before the Commissioners for the Purposes of this Act as aforesaid, or in case any Person appearing before the said Commissioners shall decline to answer any Question put to him or her by the said Commissioners, or being summoned shall not appear before the said Commissioners to be examined, it shall be lawful for the said Commissioners, and they are hereby required, according to the best of their Judgement, to settle and ascertain in what Sums such Person ought to be charged, and to make an Assessment accordingly: And that when and as soon as the said Commissioners shall have signed and allowed any Assessments to be made by virtue of this Act, they shall cause Copies of such Assessments, signed by

Two

Two or more of the said Commissioners, to be made out and transmitted to the respective Collectors, appointed or to be appointed as aforesaid, in each Parish or Place within the Divisions of the said respective Commissioners, and also another Copy thereof to the Commissioners for hearing and determining Appeals for the County or Place where such Assessment shall be made: And the said respective Commissioners, for the Purposes of this Act, shall issue out their Warrants to the Collectors as herein-after is required, according as the same shall become payable, at the Expiration of Seven Days after signing and allowing the said Assessments; and the Collectors, to whom a Copy of such Assessment shall be delivered, shall forthwith cause Notice in Writing of the Amount of each Person's Assessment to be given to the Person or Persons respectively charged, or left at his or her last or usual Place of Residence in the Parish or Place for which such Assessment shall have been made, in pursuance of this Act.

the Assessment to the Party charged.

LXIV. And be it further enacted, That if any Person or Persons shall think him, her, or themselves aggrieved by any Rate or Assessment to be made by virtue of this Act; or if in any Case where a Schedule shall have been delivered, and a subsequent Examination shall have taken place as herein-before directed, (except where the Party or Parties to be charged shall have verified his, her, or their

Persons aggrieved by Assessments, and Surveyors dissatisfied with the Determination of the Commissioners, on a Schedule delivered, (except where it is verified on Oath), may

E

appeal; the Surveyor, within 40 Days after the Affeffment made, and the Party with n 14 Days after Notice thereof, (but not afterwards, unlefs on fpecial Caufe fhewn) to the Commiffioners of Appeal, giving 10 Days Notice.

their Schedule, or fhall have anfwered on Oath or Affirmation all fuch Queftions as fhall have been demanded of him, her, or them, by the faid refpective Commiffioners), any Surveyor or Infpector fhall be diffatisfied with the Determination of the faid Commiffioners for the Purpofes of this Act, it fhall be lawful for fuch Surveyor or Infpector, within Forty Days after fuch Affeffment fhall be made, and for fuch Party or Parties refpectively, within Fourteen Days after Notice of any Affeffment made upon him, her, or them, by virtue of this Act, fhall have been given or left as aforefaid, but not afterwards, unlefs fpecial Caufe be fhewn to the Satisfaction of the Commiffioners of Appeals as herein is mentioned, to appeal to the Commiffioners appointed to hear and determine Appeals for the County, Riding, Shire, Stewartry, or Place where the Matter of fuch Appeal fhall arife, giving Ten Days Notice thereof at the leaft to the faid Commiffioners; And the faid laft mentioned Commiffioners

The faid Commiffioners may fummon the Party charged, and Witneffes;

may, on any fuch Appeal being entered, fummon any Perfon or Perfons, either on the Part of the Party or Parties affeffed, or any other Perfon or Perfons whom the faid Commiffioners fhall judge able to give them Information refpecting the Particulars mentioned in fuch Schedule, or on fuch other Points as they fhall think neceffary for afcertaining the due Proportions which fuch Party or Parties affeffed ought to pay by virtue of this Act; And the faid laft mentioned Commiffioners

miffioners are hereby authorized and required to hear and determine all fuch Appeals duly made within the Time before limited, and to make fuch Amendment in the Affeffment of the Party appealing or appealed againft, either by increafing or diminifhing the Sum affeffed, as to the faid Commiffioners fhall, under all Circumftances proved to them, appear juft and equitable : Provided always, That where the Party affeffed appeals from fuch Affeffment, or in cafe of an Appeal by the Surveyor or Infpector where the Party appealed againft fhall not have delivered a Schedule to the Commiffioners for the Purpofes of this Act, fuch Party fhall, Ten Days at leaft previous to the hearing of fuch Appeal, deliver, or caufe to be delivered, to the faid laft mentioned Commiffioners, or their Clerk, having taken the Oath hereinbefore prefcribed, a Schedule of Particulars, in Writing, of his, her, or their Income, according to the Form in the Schedule to this Act annexed, marked (D.); and the faid Commiffioners fhall not be at Liberty to relieve from the faid Affeffment, or to make any Abatement therein, unlefs the Party or Parties affeffed fhall, at the Time of hearing fuch Appeal, verify the Schedule of Particulars delivered by him, her, or them, either on Oath or Affirmation taken before the faid Commiffioners, or on Affidavit made and taken according to the Directions of this Act, nor unlefs the Party or Parties affeffed, or fuch Agent, Clerk, or Servant of fuch

and on hearing the Appeal, may amend the Affeffment.

If the Party affeffed appeal, (or the Surveyor, etc. where no Schedule is delivered), he muft, 10 Days at leaft before the Hearing, deliver to the Commiffioners of Appeal or their fworn Clerk, a Schedule of his Income; but no Relief fhall be afforded him, unlefs he verify the Schedule on Oath, nor unlefs he, or his Agent, fhall anfwer all Queftions afked, and produce all Writings, etc. demanded by the Commiffioners.

E 2　　　　　Party

Party or Parties affeffed, as the faid Commiffioners fhall require to be examined, or
fome credible Witnefs or Witneffes on the
Behalf of fuch Party or Parties affeffed,
fhall, to the Satisfaction of the faid Commiffioners, anfwer all fuch Queftions, and produce fuch Conveyances, Inftruments, Writings, and Documents, relative to the Income
of fuch Party or Parties affeffed, as the
Commiffioners fhall judge neceffary to enable them to afcertain the true Sum in which
the faid Party or Parties affeffed ought to be
charged.

Though a
Party fwear to
his Schedule,
the Surveyor
may, on de-
claring him-
felf diffatisfied
with the Com-
miffioners
Determina-
tion, demand
a Cafe from
them, to be
fent to the
Commiffion-
ers of Appeal,
according to
whofe Opi-
nion the Af-
feffment fhall
be fettled.

LXV. Provided always, and be it further
enacted, That in any Cafe where the Party
affeffed fhall have verified the Particulars
contained in his or her Schedule of Income
upon Oath, and where the Surveyor or
Infpector fhall neverthelefs apprehend the
Determination made by the faid Commiffioners to be contrary to the true Intent and
Meaning of this Act, or that they have difallowed any Surcharge, or allowed any Deduction contrary to the fame, and fhall then
declare himfelf diffatisfied with fuch Determination, it fhall and may be lawful for fuch
Surveyor or Infpector to require the faid
Commiffioners to ftate fpecially and fign the
Cafe upon which the Queftion arofe, together with their Determination thereupon;
which Cafe the faid Commiffioners, or the
major Part of them then prefent, are hereby
required to ftate and fign accordingly, and

To caufe the fame to be by him tranfmitted to the Commiffioners of Appeal, who are hereby required, with all convenient Speed, to return an Anfwer to the Cafe fo tranfmitted, with their Opinion thereupon fubfcribed thereto, according to which Opinion fo certified, the Affeffment, which fhall have been the Caufe of fuch Appeal, fhall be altered or confirmed.

LXVI. Provided always, and be it further enacted, That if Appeal fhall be made by virtue of this Act on the Behalf of any Perfon or Perfons who fhall be abfent out of the Realm, or be prevented by Sicknefs or other fufficient Caufe from attending in Perfon the hearing of fuch Appeal, it fhall be lawful for the Commiffioners for hearing and determining fuch Appeal to poftpone from Time to Time the hearing of fuch Appeal, or to admit other Proof of the Schedule than the Oath or Affirmation of fuch Party, if the faid Commiffioners fhall be fatisfied of the Truth of the Reafon alledged for fuch Delay or Admiffion of other Proof: And further, That it fhall alfo be lawful for the faid Commiffioners to direct the levying of the Sum fo affeffed to be ftayed until the Determination of the Appeal poftponed for any Caufe before mentioned.

In Appeals on Behalf of Perfons Abroad, or prevented from attending by Sicknefs, etc. the Commiffioners may poftpone the Hearing, or admit other Proof of the Schedule than the Party's Oath; and may ftop the levying of the Sum affeffed.

LXVII. And be it further enacted, That if any Perfon required in purfuance of this Act to make out and deliver any Lift, Statement,

Perfons refufing or neglecting to make out and deliver Lifts and State-

E 3

ments re-
quired, to
forfeit not ex-
ceeding 20l.

ment, or Schedule herein deſcribed, ſhall
neglect or refuſe to make out and ſign ſuch
Liſt, Statement, and Schedule, or either of
them, as the Caſe may require, and deliver
or cauſe the ſame to be delivered to the Aſ-
ſeſſor or Aſſeſſors within the Time herein
mentioned, he or ſhe ſo refuſing or offending
ſhall, for every ſuch Default or Offence, forfeit a Sum not exceeding the Sum of Twenty
Pounds, to be recovered as any Penalty may
be recovered under the ſaid Act, or this
Act.

Commiſſion-
ers under this
Act ſhall be
aſſeſſe I by the
Commiſſion-
ers of Appeal;
and the State-
ments deli-
vered by Com-
miſſioners,
ſhall be tranſ-
mitted to the
Commiſſion-
ers of Ap-
peal, who
ſhall act in all
ſuch Reſpects
as Commiſ-
ſioners do in
others ; Cer-
tificates of
ſuch Aſſeſſ-
ments ſhall be
tranſmitted to
the Commiſ-
ſioners, to be
certified and
returned, and
the Aſſeſſment
levied and

LXVIII. And be it further enacted, That
the Commiſſioners for hearing and determining Appeals, in any County, Riding, Shire,
Stewartry, or Place, ſhall aſſeſs all and every
the Commiſſioners for the Purpoſes of this
Act, within the ſame County, Riding, Shire,
Stewartry, or Place ; or within any City,
Town, or Pace being a County of itſelf,
ſituate within ſuch County, Riding, Shire,
Stewartry, or Place : And whenever any Liſt
or Statement ſhall be delivered in purſuance
of this Act by any ſuch Commiſſioner for
the Purpoſes thereof, or on his Behalf, or
on his Default, ſuch Liſt or Statement ſhall
be forthwith tranſmitted to the Commiſſioners for hearing and determining Appeals for
ſuch County, Riding, Shire, Stewartry, or
Place, who ſhall have Authority, and are
hereby required to aſſeſs and determine the
Sum which ſuch Commiſſioner ought to contribute in purſuance of this Act: And ſuch
Com-

Commiffioners for hearing and determining *collected, as in other Cafes.* Appeals fhall and may act in all Refpects therein in the fame Manner, and have and ufe the fame Powers and Authorities in all Refpects therein, as the Commiffioners for the Purpofes of this Act can or may act, and have and ufe, in Cafes of other Perfons having any Income, chargeable by virtue of this Act: Provided always, That the faid Commiffioners for hearing and determining Appeals fhall tranfmit, or caufe to be tranf-mitted, a Certificate of the Affeffment fo to be made to the Commiffioners for the Pur-pofes of this Act, in order that the Amount thereof may be certified in the Duplicates of Affeffments to be made out and returned in purfuance of this Act, and collected and levied accordingly.

LXIX. And be it further enacted, That if any Commiffioner for the Purpofes of this Act fhall think himfelf aggrieved by any Rate or Affeffment to be made by the faid Commiffioners for hearing and determining Appeals by virtue of this Act; or if any Commiffioner for hearing and determining Appeals fhall think himfelf aggrieved by the Rate or Affeffment to be made by the faid Commiffioners for the Purpofes of this Act; it fhall and may be lawful for fuch refpec-tive Commiffioner, within Fourteen Days af-ter Notice of any fuch Affeffment made upon him by virtue of this Act, to appeal to the Commiffioners for hearing and determining Appeals to be appointed in and for fome

If Commif-fioners or Commiffion-ers of Appeal think them-felves aggriev-ed by the Af-feffment made on them by each other re-fpectively, they may ap-peal againft the fame to Commiffion-ers of Appeal for fome ad-joining Coun-ty, etc.

County,

County, Riding, Shire, or Stewartry imme‑ diately adjoining the County, Riding, Shire, or Stewartry, where such Cause of Appeal shall arise, at the Election of the Party preferring such Appeal: And it shall be lawful for the said last mentioned Commissioners of Appeal to hear and determine the Matter so referred to them, in the same Manner, in all Respects, as if the Cause of Appeal had arisen in the County, Riding, Shire, or Stewartry for which they shall be so appointed Commis‑ sioners of Appeal as aforesaid.

Commission‑ ers shall not vote on any disputed Point in Cases of In‑ come, in which they are interested, either directly, or as Trus‑ tees; and if there be not Two disinte‑ rested Com‑ missioners, the Question may be determined by Commis‑ sioners of an adjoining Di‑ vision, etc.

LXX. Provided always, and be it further enacted, That in case any Differences or Dis‑ putes shall arise between the said Commis‑ sioners for the Purposes of this Act, or be‑ tween the Commissioners for hearing and determining Appeals, respecting the Rates or Assessments to be made by virtue of this Act, in respect of Income arising from any Pro‑ perty wherein any of the said respective Com‑ missioners shall or may be concerned or inte‑ rested, or shall be Trustee, Agent, Receiver, Guardian, Committee, or Curator, to any Person so concerned or interested, the Com‑ missioner who shall be so concerned or inte‑ rested in such Rate or Assessment, or shall be such Trustee, Agent, Receiver, Guardian, Committee, or Curator, shall have no Voice, but shall withdraw until it shall be deter‑ mined by the Rest of the Commissioners; and if there shall not be Two Commissioners not interested as aforesaid, then the Matter in Dispute shall be determined by Commission‑

ers

ers acting in any adjoining Division, or, where the Case shall require the same, in any adjoining County, Riding, Shire, or Stewartry.

LXXI. And be it further enacted, That if the said Commissioners shall disallow the Application of any Surveyor or Inspector to proceed upon any Surcharge, or upon any Representation or Certificate of any erroneous Assessment, it shall be lawful for such Surveyor or Inspector, or any Surveyor or Inspector to be appointed in his Stead, to appeal against the Decision of such Commissioners to the Commissioners of Appeal, and to require the Judgement of the said Commissioners of Appeal whether there is sufficient Reason to proceed upon such Surcharge or Representation: And in case the said Commissioners of Appeal shall be of Opinion that there is sufficient Reason to proceed upon such Surcharge or Representation, they shall refer the Matter back to the Commissioners who originally decided thereon; and such Commissioners shall, according to the Direction of such Commissioners of Appeal, proceed upon the Application of such Surveyor or Inspector, in such Manner as they would have done if they had originally decided in the same Manner as the said Commissioners of Appeal shall have thought fit to direct.

If Commissioners in any Case disallow Application of a Surveyor, etc. he or his Successor may resort to the Commissioners of Appeal, and if they determine in his Favour, they shall refer back to the Commissioners, to act as if they had originally allowed such Application.

LXXII. And be it further enacted, That the First Assessment to be made by virtue of this Act shall be made for One Year, at the respective

The First Assessment shall be made for One Year

from *April* 5, 1799, to *April* 5, 18co, and fo in every fubfequent Year; payable by Six equal Inftalments, the Firft on the 5th *June*; and to be paid within 10 Days of each Day of Inftalment.

refpective Rates before mentioned, from the Fifth Day of *April* One thoufand feven hundred and ninety-nine, until the Fifth Day of *April* One thoufand eight hundred; and every fubfequent Affeffment fhall be made for One Year, from the Fifth Day of *April* yearly: And the feveral Sums affeffed by any fuch Affeffment fhall be payable in Six Inftalments at the Times following; *videlicet*, the Fifth Day of *June*, the Fifth Day of *Auguft*, the Fifth Day of *October*, the Fifth Day of *December*, the Fifth Day of *February*, and the Fifth Day of *April* yearly, by even and equal Portions: The Firft of the faid Inftalments to be payable on the Fifth Day of *June* One thoufand feven hundred and ninety-nine; and the Payments fhall be made within Ten Days from the Day when the fame fhall be payable by virtue of

Warrants to be iffued by Commiffioners for levying the fame; and all Arrears to be Debts of Record to the King.

this Act: And it fhall be lawful for the refpective Commiffioners for the Purpofes of this Act to iffue out and deliver to the Collectors appointed to collect the Duties on Houfes, Windows, or Lights, or any other the Duties under the Management of the Commiffioners for the Affairs of Taxes for the Time being, their Warrants for the fpeedy collecting and levying the faid Rates, as the fame fhall become payable, by Six Inftalments, commencing in each Year from the Fifth Day of *April* yearly, according to the true Intent and Meaning of this Act: And that fuch Part thereof as cannot be fo levied and collected, fhall be recoverable as a Debt upon Record

to

to the King's Majesty, His Heirs and Succeffors.

LXXIII. And be it further enacted, That
every Houfeholder and Occupier as aforefaid fhall be liable to be charged to the Rate
hereby granted, in the Parifh or Place of his
or her Refidence, at the Time of the Execution of this Act, in giving general Notice
as herein required, in refpect of the Whole
of his or her Income chargeable by virtue of
this Act, although fuch Perfon fhall have
Property, or fhall exercife or carry on any
Profeffion, Office, Employment, Trade, or
Vocation, or fhall receive any Penfion or
Stipend, in any other Parifh or Place, unlefs
fuch Perfon fhall have another Place or Places
of ordinary Refidence in fome other Parifh
or Place, or Parifhes or Places, and fhall
give Notice thereof in Manner herein-after
mentioned : And that every Affeffment made
upon any Perfon as a Truftee, Agent, or
Receiver, Guardian, Tutor, Curator, or Committee, on the Behalf of any other Perfon or
Perfons, or upon any Chamberlain, Treafurer,
Clerk, or other Officer, acting as Treafurer,
Auditor, or Receiver, for the Time being,
of any Corporation, Company, Fraternity,
or Society as aforefaid, on the Behalf of fuch
Corporation, Company, Fraternity, or Society, fhall alfo be charged in the Parifh or
Place where fuch Truftee, Agent, Receiver,
Guardian, Tutor, Curator, or Committee,
or fuch Chamberlain, Treafurer, Clerk, or

other

Every Houfe- holder, &c. fhall be charg- ed to the Rate on the Whole of his Income, in his Place of Refidence, at the Time of the General Notice under this Act, [fee § 44], unlefs he refides elfe- where [fee the next §.] Every Affeffment made on a Truftee, or on any Officer of a Corpora- tion, fhall be charged in the Place where fuch Truftee, etc. fo refides ; all Perfons not being Houfe- holders fhall be charged at their Place of actual Refi- dence ; and the Affeffment fhall remain valid notwith- ftanding their Removal, un- lefs on Notice. Perfons out of the Realm fhall be rated at their laft Place of Re- fidence if known; or where their Property is; unlefs on Defire of their Agent to be affeffed elfewhere.

other Officer as aforefaid, fhall refide at the Time of the Commencement of the Execution of this Act in each Year, unlefs Notice of his or her ordinary Refidence in fome other Parifh or Place fhall be given as herein is directed: And all Perfons not being Houfeholders or Occupiers as aforefaid, nor having a certain Place of Refidence, fhall be charged at the Place where they fhall be refident at the Time of the Execution of this Act as aforefaid: And every fuch Charge made in the Parifh or Place of fuch Refidence, at the Time of the Execution of this Act as laft aforefaid, fhall be valid and effectual, notwithftanding the fubfequent Removal of any fuch Perfon from fuch Parifh or Place, unlefs a Noticethereof fhall be given to the Affeffors as herein-after is directed: And if any Perfon who ought to be charged by virtue of this Act fhall, at the Time of his or her Affeffment, be out of the Realm, fuch Perfon fhall be rated for the fame in fuch Parifh or Place where he or fhe was laft ordinarily refident, or abiding within this Realm, if the fame fhall be known, or otherwife, where he or fhe fhall have any Property, unlefs his or her Agent or Receiver fhall be defirous of being affeffed in any other Place, and fhall give Notice thereof in Manner herein-after mentioned.

Perfons refiding in any other Parifh than where

LXXIV. And be it further enacted, That every Perfon ordinarily refiding in any other Parifh or Place than the Parifh or

Place

Place of his or her Refidence at the Time of Service of Notice to him or her, or to the Houfeholder of the Dwelling Houfe where fuch Perfon did refide at the Time of fuch Service, or at the Time of fuch general Notice as aforefaid, and every Perfon removing from the Parifh or Place where he or fhe did refide at the Time of fuch Service, being refpectively defirous not to be charged in fuch Parifh or Place, fhall give Notice thereof to the Affeffors of the faid Parifh or Place, or One of them ; and if any Perfon fhall remove from the Parifh or Place of his or her Refidence without giving fuch Notice, and with Intent to evade the Payment of the Rates hereby granted, every fuch Perfon fhall forfeit and pay the Sum of Fifty Pounds, to be recovered as any Penalty may be recovered under the faid firft-recited Act; and the Removal fhall not in fuch Cafe affect the Affeffment to be made in the Parifh or Place of fuch his or her laft Refidence.

they receive Notice, or removing from thence, fhall give Notice of their Removal to an Affeffor: Removing without Notice with Intent to evade the Duties, fhall incur the Penalty of 50l. and the Affeffment fhall remain in force.

LXXV. Provided always, and be it further enacted, That every Perfon having Two or more Dwelling Houfes, and refiding in different Divifions of Commiffioners for the Purpofes of this Act, fhall, in each of fuch Divifions, be required to deliver, in Manner before directed, a Statement of the whole Sum which he or fhe is willing to contribute, or a Declaration in lieu thereof, declaring in what other Place he or fhe is defirous

Perfons refiding in different Divifions fhall deliver a Statement of their propofed Contribution in each, or a Declaration in what other Place they are to be charged; and may elect either to pay the

Whole in one Division, or in proportionate Parts in both Divisions: If they neglect to give a proper Statement or Declaration, &c they may be charged in each Division, but relievable on Appeal, and making such Election.

firous of being charged; and such Person may, at the Time of delivering such Statement or Declaration, elect to pay the Whole of the Rate in either of such Divisions, on giving Notice in Writing of such his or her Intention to the respective Assessors within the Parishes or Places where such Dwelling Houses are situate, or may elect to pay the same by Payments to be made in different Divisions, in such Proportions as the Party shall in such Notices express: Provided that if in any such Case no Statement shall be delivered, or a Declaration in lieu thereof, nor any Notice shall be given as before directed, at the Time of the Delivery of any Statement, then and in every such Case, an Assessment upon the Whole of the Income of such Person shall be made in each Division where such Dwelling Houses are situated: Provided that any Person who shall be overrated by reason thereof shall be relieved therefrom, upon Appeal, on Proof before the respective Commissioners, of the Amount of such Overcharge upon such Appellant, and upon his or her making an Election where the Rates which ought to be charged upon such Person shall be paid.

If a Person assessed in one Parish shall be again assessed in another, the Commissioners where he pays

LXXVI. Provided always, and be it further enacted, That if any Person or Persons, having been assessed in any Parish or Place for his or her Income, shall be again assessed in any other Parish or Place in respect of the same Income, in every such Case the Commissioners

missioners for the Purposes of this Act, acting for the Parish or Place where such Person or Persons shall elect to pay his, her, or their Contribution, or Two of them at the least, shall, on any Application for that Purpose, grant a Certificate of such Assessment, signed by them, *gratis*: And upon Proof of such Assessment before the Commissioners acting for such other Parish or Place, either by the Production of such Certificate, or in Default thereof by other Evidence to their Satisfaction, the said last mentioned Commissioners shall cause the Assessment of such Person or Persons so again assessed to be amended or vacated, as the Case may require, so that such Person or Persons shall not be charged more than by this Act he, she, or they ought to be charged.

shall grant him a Certificate thereof, and the other Assessment shall be vacated.

LXXVII. And in order that the Estimates of Annual Income chargeable by virtue of this Act may be made according to known Rules, and with as much Uniformity as the respective Cases will admit, be it further enacted, That in all Cases the Income chargeable by virtue of this Act shall be estimated according to the Rules and Directions prescribed by this Act, and the Schedule hereunto annexed, as far as the same respectively are applicable to such Income; and in all Cases where the same are not applicable, then according to the best of the Knowledge and Belief of the Person whose Duty it shall be to estimate or compute

Income shall in all Cases be estimated according to the Directions of this Act and the Schedule annexed, or according to the best of the Knowledge and Belief of the Party.

pute such Income, whether such Estimate
shall be made by any Person chargeable by
virtue of this Act, on his or her own Account, or on the Account of any other, or
as an Officer in the Execution of his Duty,
as prescribed by this Act: But that it shall
not be lawful, in computing such Income,
to make any other or greater Deductions
therefrom than such as are expressly enume-
rated in this Act, or in the Schedule hereunto annexed, nor to make any Deductions
which by the Schedule or the Act are directed not to be made.

Where Income is diminished by any specifick Cause, Commissioners may allow an Abatement.

LXXVIII. Provided always, and be it
further enacted, That if any Person shall
prove, to the Satisfaction of the respective
Commissioners before-mentioned, that his or
her Income chargeable by virtue of this Act
has been diminished from any specifick Cause
arising after the Time when such Income
ought to be computed according to this Act,
it shall be lawful for the said respective
Commissioners to make such Abatement as
to them shall seem just in respect of such
Diminution of Income.

Income arising from a Profession, Office, &c. shall be estimated either according to the actual Produce in the preceding Year, or

LXXIX. And be it further enacted, That
any Income arising from any Profession,
Office, Pension, Stipend, Employment,
Trade, or Vocation, shall be estimated either
according to the actual Produce of the same
Profession, Office, Pension, Stipend, Employment, Trade, or Vocation, in the Year
immediately

immediately preceding such Estimate, or by an Average of the Produce of the Three Years immediately preceding, at the Option of the Party to be charged in respect thereof, and subject to Diminution within the current Year, in the Manner provided by the said recited Act, every such Year ending on the Thirty-first Day of *December* in each Year, or at such Time of the Year as the Accounts of such Income have been usually made up or completed for that Year, or the same had been received.

on the Average Produce of Three Years preceding, in the Option of the Party, subject to Diminution within the current Year. [See Schedule A. 15th Case.]

LXXX. And be it further enacted, That where in any Case the Income of any Person or Persons, or any Part thereof, in whatever Manner arising, shall be estimated upon any Average of Years according to the Directions of this Act, such Person or Persons shall not be entitled to any Abatement or Allowance in the current or any subsequent Year, by reason of any Variation in the Amount of the Income so arising, nor for any specifick Cause, other than in such Cases where such Person or Persons shall cease to be possessed of the Property, Office, Pension, or Stipend, or shall cease to be engaged in the Profession, Trade, or Employment, from which such Income, or Part of Income, shall have arisen.

Where Income is estimated on an Average of Years, no Abatement shall be allowed in the current Year, except where the Party shall cease to be possessed of the Property, or to be engaged in the Profession whence his Income arises.

LXXXI. And be it further enacted, That it shall not be lawful for any Persons engaged in any Trade or Manufacture, in filling

No Deduction shall be made from the Income of Traders, &c. for Sums em-

F

ployed in Im-
provements,
or as Capital,
or as Interest
of Capital,
(except where
actually paid
to another),
nor for Re-
pairs, Imple-
ments, &c.
beyond the
Average of
the Three
preceding
Years, nor
from Property
not employed
as Capital by
Reason of any
Diminution
of Capital.

ling up the Statement or Schedule of the
Particulars of their Income, or on otherwise
computing, in pursuance of this Act, their
Income arising from such Trade or Manufacture, to make any Deductions therefrom
on Account of any Sums employed, or intended to be employed, in Improvements or
as Capital, or on Account of Interest for
the Capital by them employed therein, unlefs for Interest, which they are bound to
pay to other Perfons for the fame; nor for
any Sum expended by them in the Course
of any One Year (in which the Estimate or
Average thereof shall be taken) for Repairs
of Premises occupied for the Purpose of such
Trade or Manufacture, or for the Supply, or
Repairs, or Alterations of any Implements
or Utensils, or Articles employed for the
Purpose of such Trade or Manufacture, beyond the Amount of the Sum usually expended for such Purposes, according to an
Average of Three Years preceding the Year
to which such Computation shall relate; nor
shall it be lawful for any Person engaged in
Trade or Manufacture, and having Property
not employed as Capital therein, to make
any Deduction from the Income arising from
the Property not employed as Capital, by
reason of any Diminution of the Capital so
employed, during the Period for which such
Computation shall be made.

Partners may
be jointly
charged in

LXXXII. Provided always, and be it further enacted, That any Perfons engaged in
any

any Trade or Manufacture, or in any Adventure or Concern, in Partnership together, may be jointly charged to the said Rates and Duties, in respect of their Joint Income arising from such Trade or Manufacture, or such Adventure or Concern; under the Firm or Description of their said Business; and that the Return of any One of the said Partners, on Behalf of himself and the others for that Purpose; shall be sufficient Authority for the said Commissioners to charge such Partners jointly in respect of their Income arising from such Trade or Manufacture, or such Adventure or Concern, but nevertheless wholly distinct from any Charge which may be made upon such Persons, or any of them, in respect of any other Income belonging to them, or any of them.

respect of their Joint Incomes, and the Return of One Partner shall be sufficient; such Charge shall be distinct from that on their separate Incomes.

LXXXIII. And be it further enacted, That if amongst any Persons engaged in Trade or Manufacture, in Partnership together, any Change shall take place in any such Partnership, either by Death or Dissolution of Partnership, as to all or any of the Partners, or by admitting any other Partner therein, within the Period when the Computation of Income ought to be made under this Act, or before the Time of making the Assessment under this Act; or if any Person shall have succeeded to any Trade or Manufacture, or any Adventure or Concern, within such respective Periods as aforesaid; it shall be lawful for the said respective Commissioners,

In case of Changes in Partnership, the Charges on the Partnership, and on the Partners going out or coming in, shall remain the same; unless a specifick Cause for Diminution is shewn to the Commissioners.

F 2

fioners, and they, and alfo the Party or Parties interefted, and every Officer acting in
the Execution of this Act, fhall compute and
afcertain the Income of fuch Partnerfhip, or
any of fuch Partners, or any Perfon fucceeding to fuch Trade or Manufacture, or Adventure or Concern, according to the Income
derived during the refpective Periods before-
mentioned, notwithftanding fuch Change
therein or Succeffion to fuch Bufinefs as
aforefaid, unlefs fuch Partners or Partner, or
fuch Perfon fucceeding to fuch Bufinefs as
aforefaid, fhall prove, to the Satisfaction of
the faid refpective Commiffioners, that the
Income of fuch Perfon or Perfons hath fallen
fhort, or will fall fhort, for fome fpecifick
Caufe to be alledged to them, fince fuch
Change or Succeffion took place, or by reafon
thereof.

Where the
Title to In-
come is un-
certain, or in
Difpute, the
actual Re-
ceiver fhall
give a State-
ment thereof,
and pay the
Duty thereon;
and Courts of
Equity may
give the pro-
per Directions,
on Applica-
tion of Truf-
tees, as to
Property un-
der their Con-
troul.

LXXXIV. And be it further enacted,
That in all Cafes in which the Title to any
Income fhall be uncertain, either by reafon
of any Contingency to which the fame may
be fubject, or by reafon of any Difpute concerning the fame, or for any other Caufe,
then fuch Income fhall be chargeable under
this Act feparately, according to the Amount
thereof, and the Perfon or Perfons (if any)
who fhall be in the Receipt of fuch Income,
whether on his or her own Account, or on
the Behalf of any other Perfon or Perfons,
fhall deliver a Statement thereof accordingly,
and fhall pay the Sums chargeable in refpect
thereof

thereof out of fuch Income: And in cafe fuch Income fhall be under the Controul or Direction of any Court of Equity, or other Court, in any Suit depending, or otherwife, fuch Court fhall give the neceffary Directions for afcertaining the Amount of fuch Income, and Payment of the Duty chargeable thereon, upon Application in a fummary Way of any Truftee or Truftees, or any Perfon or Perfons interefted therein, or any Agent or Receiver intrufted with the Receip thereof, or of any Surveyor or Infpector acting in the Execution of this Act.

LXXXV. And be it further enacted, That all Income belonging to any Infant, or other Perfon or Perfons, which fhall be under the Direction or Controul of any Court of Equity or other Court, in any Suit depending or otherwife, fhall be charged and affeffed, under the Direction of fuch Court, in all Cafes in which fuch Income cannot be otherwife charged and affeffed under this Act; and fuch Court fhall give all neceffary Directions for fuch Purpofe, and for Payment of the Duties which fhall be fo charged and affeffed, in the fame Manner as is herein-before directed with refpect to Income under the Controul of any Court, the Title whereto fhall be uncertain.

Income of Infants, under the Controul of Courts of Equity, &c. fhall be affeffed, and the Duty paid thereon under the Direction of fuch Court.

LXXXVI. And be it further enacted, That all Proceedings in any Court, for the Purpofe of charging any fuch Income as aforefaid,

Proceedings in fuch Cafes fhall be free of Stamp Duty.

aforefaid, and obtaining Payment of the Duties chargeable thereon, fhall be free of Stamp Duties, and all Fees and Charges attending the fame, except for Writing.

Revenues of Corporations, etc. not appiicable to charitable Purpofes, fhall be charged as other Incomes.

LXXXVII. And be it further enacted, That where any Bodies Politick or Corporate, Companies, Fraternities, or Societies of Perfons, whether Corporate or not Corporate, fhall be entitled unto any Annual Income to the refpective Amounts before fpecified, (other than and befides any Income applicable to charitable Purpofes), fuch Annual Income (not applicable to charitable Purpofes only) fhall be chargeable with fuch and the like Rates as any other Annual Income of the fame Amount will, under and by virtue of this Act, be chargeable with.

No Corporation, &c. fhall be chargeable in refpect of Income applicable to charitable Purpofes, nor the Dividends on which are paid to individual Members : Such Dividends fhall be chargeabie in the Hands of the Perfon entitled thereto as they are payable, except Dividends

LXXXVIII. Provided always, and be it further enacted, That no fuch Bodies Politick or Corporate, Companies, Fraternities, or Societies aforefaid, fhall be charged or chargeable, in refpect of any Income, which, according to the Rules or Regulations of fuch Corporations, Companies, Fraternities, or Societies, fhall be applicable to charitable Purpofes, or to the Payment of any Annual Dividends or Intereft to arife and become payable to any individual Members of fuch Corporations or Publick Companies, or to any other Perfons or Publick Bodies, having any Share, Right, or Title of, in, or to any Capital Stock, or other Property belonging

to

to such Corporations or Publick Companies, nor in respect of which any Dividends or Interest shall, according to such Rules and Regulations, become payable: Provided that such Person or Persons, Corporations, Companies, Fraternities, or Societies, to whom such Dividends or Interest shall be payable, shall be charged and chargeable in respect thereof, according to the Amounts thereof, and the Rates before specified, as and when the same shall be received by them respectively, (other than and except Dividends and Interest the Property of Persons not the Subjects of His Majesty, and not resident in this Kingdom,) and that an Account of the Amount of such Dividends and Interest be delivered to such Inspector or Surveyor as shall be authorized for that Purpose under the Hands of Three or more of the Commissioners for the Affairs of Taxes, upon Demand thereof, by the same Persons, and in the same Manner, as the Statements of the Income of such Corporations, Companies, Fraternities, and Societies, are required to be delivered.

payable to Foreigners not resident in this Kingdom; the Amount of which is to be delivered to an Inspector, &c. in the same Manner as Statements of Income under this Act.

LXXXIX. Provided also, and be it further enacted, That no Corporate City, Borough, Town, or Place, shall be liable to be charged in respect of such Portion of the Income belonging to such Corporation as shall be appropriated by any Act, Statute, or Bye Law, towards defraying the Expences incident to the Civil Government of such Corporation;

No Corporate City, &c. shall be charged for Income appropriated to the Expences of its Government, nor Collegiate Bodies, etc. for Income applied to the

Maintenance of Fellows, *etc.* but the Accounts ſhall be made up annually, and the Parties benefited ſhall be charged.

poration; and that no Body Politick, Corporate, or Collegiate, ſhall be liable to be charged in reſpect of ſuch Part of its Income which, by virtue of any Private Statutes or Charter, or of any Will or other Inſtrument of Endowment belonging to or for the Eſtabliſhment or Confirmation of the Conſtitution of ſuch Body Politick, Corporate, or Collegiate, ſhall be appropriated to the Maintenance, Subſiſtence, or Advancement of any Maſters, Fellows, Students, or Members thereof: Provided that in every Caſe where ſuch Exemption ſhall be claimed, an Account thereof ſhall be made up in the uſual Form for each Year during the Term herein mentioned and allowed by the ſaid Commiſſioners, and that the Perſons to whoſe Uſe ſuch Income ſhall be applied, ſhall be chargeable in reſpect thereof, as in other Caſes under this Act.

The proper Officer of Corporations within 28 Days of each General Notice ſhall deliver to the Inſpector, &c. a Statement of the annual Income of ſuch Corporation, according to the Form in Schedule B, ſpecifying what Part

XC. And be it further enacted, That the Chamberlain, Treaſurer, Clerk, or other Officer acting as Treaſurer, Auditor, or Receiver, for the Time being, of every ſuch Corporation, Company, Fraternity, or Society, ſhall and he is hereby required, within Twenty-eight Days after the Publication of ſuch general Notice as herein mentioned, in the Pariſh or Place wherein the Office of ſuch Chamberlain, Treaſurer, Clerk, or other Officer, ſhall be ſituate, to make out and deliver to the Inſpector or Surveyor duly authorized as aforeſaid, a Statement of the

Annual

Annual Income of fuch Corporation, Company, Fraternity, or Society, according to the Form fpecified in the Schedule to this Act annexed, marked (B.); and fhall alfo fpecify in fuch Statement how much and what Proportion of fuch Annual Income is not chargeable by virtue of this Act upon fuch Corporation, Company, Fraternity, or Society, and for what Purpofes the Income, not chargeable as aforefaid, is or fhall be applicable: And fuch Infpectors or Surveyors are hereby required to tranfmit fuch Statement to the refpective Clerks to the Commiffioners for the Purpofes of this Act, in the Manner herein directed as to Statements of Houfeholders and others charged to the faid Rates by virtue of this Act.

of fuch Income is not chargeable; fuch Statements to be tranfmitted by the Infpector, etc. to the Commiffioners Clerks.

XCI. And be it further enacted, That where any Perfon being Truftee, Agent, or Receiver, Guardian, Tutor, Curator, or Committee, of or for any Perfon or Perfons having any Income which fhall be chargeable by virtue of this Act, or any Chamberlain, Treafurer, Clerk, or other Officer of any Corporation, Company, Fraternity, or Society, having any fuch Income as aforefaid, fhall be affeffed, by virtue of this Act, to contribute any Sum or Sums in refpect of fuch Income, then and in every fuch Cafe it fhall be lawful for every fuch Perfon who fhall be fo affeffed, by and out of fuch Annual Income as fhall come to his or her Hands or Hand as fuch Truftee, Agent, or Receiver,

Guardian,

Truftees and Officers of Corporations affeffed, may retain the Amount of Duties out of Truft Monies, etc. coming to their Hands; and fhall be indemnified for all Payments made under this Act.

Guardian, Tutor, Committee, or Curator as aforesaid, or as such Chamberlain, Treasurer, Clerk, or other Officer, to retain so much and such Part of such Annual Income as shall from Time to Time be sufficient to pay such Assessment: And every such Trustee, Agent, or Receiver, Guardian, Tutor, Committee, or Curator, Chamberlain, Treasurer, Clerk, or other Officer, shall be, and they are hereby respectively indemnified against all and every Person and Persons, Corporations, Companies, Fraternities, or Societies whatsoever, for all Payments which they shall respectively make out of such Income, in pursuance and by virtue of this Act.

Persons fraudulently avoiding the being charged under this Act by changing their Place of Abode, or converting their Property, or delivering any false Account, or changing the Securities of their Property, and rendering the same unproductive, or by any Contrivance whatever, practised or to be practised, shall be charged double.

XCII. And be it further enacted, That if any Person who ought to be charged by virtue of this Act shall, by changing or having changed his or her Place of Residence, or by converting or having converted his or her Property, or any Part thereof, or by fraudulently releasing, assigning, or conveying, or having fraudulently released, assigned, or conveyed the same, or any Part thereof, or by making and delivering any such Schedule or Account as aforesaid which shall be false; or having any Property yielding an Income, shall fraudulently convert, or shall have fraudulently converted the same, or any Part thereof, by altering or having altered any Security with relation to such Property; or by fraudulently rendering or having rendered the same, or

any

any Part thereof, temporarily unproductive of such Income, in order that such Person may not be charged for the same, or any Part thereof; or by any Falsehood, Fraud, Covin, Art, or Contrivance whatsoever, already used or practised, or to be used or practised, shall not be charged and assessed according to the true Intent and Meaning of this Act; every such Person shall, on Proof thereof, before any Two or more of the said respective Commissioners, be charged and assessed, for the Purposes of this Act, Double the Amount of the Charge which ought to have been made on such Person (if no such Charge shall have been made): And if any such Charge shall have been made which shall be less than the Charge which ought to have been made on such Person, then such Person shall be assessed and charged, for the Purposes of this Act, over and above such former Charge, Double the Amount of the Difference between the Sum with which such Person shall have been charged, and the Sum with which he or she ought to have been charged.

XCIII. And be it further enacted, That where any Rate or Assessment shall have been made in pursuance of any Statement or Schedule of Income by any Person or Persons, without Examination on Oath of such Person or Persons, before the said Commissioners for the Purposes of this Act, and the said Commissioners shall at any Time, within Six Months

Where an Assessment is made on a Statement, without Examination of the Party on Oath, the Commissioners may increase the Assessment at any Time

within Six
Months, on
Notice to the
Party, who
may appeal as
in other Cafes.
Months after fuch Rate and Affeffment made,
receive Information that fuch Perfon or Perfons was or were not thereby fully affeffed
according to the Proportion of his, her, or
their Income, which ought to be contributed
in purfuance of this Act, then and in every
fuch Cafe it fhall be lawful for the faid Commiffioners, for the Purpofes of this Act, to
charge fuch Perfon or Perfons fuch Sum or
Sums of Money as, together with the Sum
before affeffed, fhall make up the full Amount
of the Sum which he, fhe, or they ought to
have contributed in purfuance of this Act;
and the faid Commiffioners fhall caufe Notice
to be given thereof to the Perfon or Perfons
who fhall be fo charged, and appoint a Day
and Time for him, her, or them, to appear
and fhew Caufe why an Affeffment fhould
not be made according to fuch Charge: And
in cafe the faid Charge fhall (after the hearing
of the Party or Parties, or in Default of his,
her, or their appearing at the Day and Time
appointed) be eftablifhed, the faid Commiffioners fhall proceed to affefs the fame upon
the Perfon or Perfons fo charged, and direct
the Manner and Proportions in which the
fame fhall be raifed: Provided always, That
it fhall be lawful for the Perfon or Perfons
who fhall be fo charged to appeal againft
fuch laft mentioned Affeffment in the fame
Manner as is herein directed in other Cafes
where an Appeal is allowed.

XCIV. And

XCIV. And be it further enacted, That if in any Inftance of Lands demifed at Rack Rent it fhall appear to the faid refpective Commiffioners, that either by reafon of fuch Lands having been let for any Term of Years more than Seven Years prior to the Year in which fuch Computation fhall be made, or for any other fpecifick Caufe to be alledged to and allowed by fuch Commiffioners, the Rules contained in the faid Schedule for eftimating the Income arifing from fuch Lands are not applicable, or will not give a fair and juft Eftimate of the Income of fuch Perfon, it fhall be lawful for fuch Commiffioners, either on the Application of the Surveyor or Infpector, or of fuch Tenant, to caufe an Affeffment to be made upon fuch Tenant in Proportion to the actual Gains and Profits received by fuch Tenant within the Year, or on an Average of Three Years preceding which fuch Computation fhall be made, and at the refpective Rates before mentioned : Provided always, That in every Inftance of Income arifing from Lands in *Scotland*, demifed at Rack Rent as aforefaid, it fhall be lawful for fuch Tenant, in making out his Statement, to compute and afcertain, and the faid refpective Commiffioners, on the Application of fuch Tenant, fhall compute and afcertain, fuch Income in Proportion to the actual Gains and Profits which fuch Tenant of Lands in *Scotland* fhall have acquired within the Year, or on an Average of Three Years preceding

If in cafe of a Tenant at Rack Rent it appears that the Rules (in Schedule A. 11th Cafe) do not apply, an Affeffment may be made (on Application of a Surveyor, or of the Tenant) on his actual Profits :

And in all Inftances of Income from Lands in Scotland let at a Rack Rent, the Tenant's Income may be ftated and computed in that Manner ; and the Commiffioners may call to their Affiftance the Information of

Occupiers and Surveyors of Land; and act as Commercial Commiffioners may do with refpect to Affiftants, under § 98.

preceding which fuch Computation fhall be made: And that when any Inquiry into the Income of any fuch Tenant fhall be to be made, the faid refpective Commiffioners may be at Liberty to call to their Affiftance any Two or more Occupiers of Lands in the fame Neighbourhood, or any Surveyor of Lands whom the faid refpective Commiffioners fhall think able to give them Affiftance in eftimating, computing, and afcertaining the Income of fuch Tenant, and upon the Refult of fuch Opinion, to require a Schedule of Particulars, and to purfue fuch Rules and Regulations for inquiring into and afcertaining the Income of fuch Tenant, as they could or might have done upon the Demand of any Surveyor or Infpector of the faid Rates and Duties, or as the Commercial Commiffioners to be appointed under this Act may lawfully do on the Advice and Affiftance of any Perfons to be called in by them for that Purpofe as herein-after mentioned.

Perfons may pay Money into the Bank, and receive Certificates, which fhall be taken as Cafh by the Collectors; but no Difcount fhall be allowed on fuch Payments.

XCV. And be it further enacted, That it fhall be lawful for any Perfon or Perfons, at any Time or Times during the Continuance of this Act, to pay, or caufe to be paid, to the Governor and Company of the Bank of *England*, or to their Cafhier or Cafhiers, any Sum or Sums of Money, and to require a Certificate or Certificates acknowledging fuch Payment; which Certificates fhall be received by the feveral Receivers and Collectors of the faid Rates and Duties as Cafh, and

and in Difcharge of fo much of the faid Rates and Duties as fhall be mentioned in fuch Certificates refpectively: Provided always, That no Difcount or Allowance whatever fhall be allowed or paid on any Sum or Sums of Money to be paid into the Bank of *England*, in purfuance of this Act.

XCVI. And be it further enacted, That in cafe any Perfon or Perfons refiding in *Great Britain*, and engaged in any Trade or Manufacture therein, or the Governor and Company of the Bank of *England*, or any other trading Body Politick or Corporate, Company, Fraternity, or Society of Perfons, whether Corporate or not Corporate, in *Great Britain*, fhall be defirous of being affeffed by the Commercial Commiffioners to be appointed as herein-after mentioned to the whole Rates and Duties granted by this Act, or to fo much thereof as may arife from Trade or Manufacture, and fhall fignify in Writing his, her, or their Intention to be fo affeffed, within the Time herein limited for returning his, her, or their Statement, to the Affeffor or Affeffors of the Parifh or Place where any Affeffment upon fuch Perfon or Perfons, Bodies, Corporations, Companies, Fraternities, or Societies, ought to be made, according to the Form marked (C.) hereunto annexed, it fhall be lawful for fuch Perfon or Perfons, by him, her, or themfelves, or his, her, or their Agent or Agents, and for fuch Bodies, Corporations,

Perfons in Trade, and the Bank and other trading Corporations, defirous to be affeffed by the Commercial Commiffioners, [fee the next and fucceeding Sections], may fignify the fame to the Affeffors according to Form (C.), within the Time for returning their Statement; and may then deliver fuch Statement to the Commercial Commiffioners of the Diftrict or their fworn Clerk, fpecifying the Branch of Trade in which fuch Parties are engaged. [For the Mode of appointing

Com-

these Commis-
fioners and
their Affiftants,
fee § 110, et
feq.]

Companies, Fraternities, or Societies; by their refpective Chamberlains, Treafurers, Cafhiers, or other Officers having the Receipt or Audit of the Income of fuch Bodies, Corporations, Companies, Fraternities, and Societies refpectively, inftead of his, her, or their delivering a Statement, as herein-before required, to the Affeffor or Affeffors for the Parifh or Place where fuch Affeffment as aforefaid ought to be made, to deliver the fame to the faid Commercial Commiffioners to be appointed for any One of the Diftricts in which fuch Affeffment is hereby directed to be made, or to their Clerk or other Officer, fworn under the Authority of this Act, who fhall be authorized by fuch refpective Commiffioners to receive the fame; and which Statements fhall be refpectively made in the Forms in the faid Schedule annexed as before directed; but neverthelefs adding thereto, by every Perfon engaged in Trade or Commerce, the particular Branch or Branches of Trade or Commerce in which fuch Perfon fhall be engaged: And the faid feveral Statements, being fo delivered, fhall be as effectual for the Purpofe of afcertaining the Sum to be affeffed on fuch Perfon or Perfons, Bodies, Corporations, Companies, Fraternities, or Societies, as if the fame had been delivered to fuch Affeffor or Affeffors in purfuance of this Act as aforefaid.

The Commer-
cial Commif-
fioners fhall

XCVII. And be it further enacted, That the refpective Commercial Commiffioners to be be appointed as herein-after directed shall, as soon after their respective Appointments as conveniently may be, meet to receive, or appoint a proper Person for receiving, all such Statements, sealed up, as shall be made to them by or on the Behalf of any Person or Persons engaged in Trade or Manufacture, and residing within the Limits of their respective Districts, or from or on the Behalf of any such Body Politick or Corporate, or Company, Fraternity, or Society of Persons within the said Limits; and shall cause all such Statements from Time to Time to be classed and registered in Books to be provided for that Purpose; and shall also from Time to Time fix a Day or Days, not sooner than Twenty-one Days from the Day of receiving any such Statement, for taking the same into Consideration; and shall from Time to Time meet for that Purpose, and may divide themselves into Committees, each Committee consisting of not less than Three Commissioners at such their Meetings; and afterwards proceed with all convenient Dispatch to ascertain and determine the Amount of the Sums to which any Person or Persons, Corporation, Company, Fraternity, or Society, delivering such Statements, ought to be charged by virtue of this Act, observing therein the Rules, Regulations, and Directions of this Act, as herein-after expressed.

receive such Statements (sealed up) and have them classed and registered in proper Books, and fix a Time within 21 Days for considering the same, and may divide themselves into Committees of Three, and assess the Parties chargeable, according to the Provisions of this Act.

Q XCVIII. And

The said Commercial Commissioners may call in Two of the Affistants, and enquire of them their Opinion of the Amount of the Income of Parties delivering in such Statements, without disclosing the Statements to such Affistants; and if such Affistants state the Income higher than the Parties have done, and Two Thirds of the Commissioners concur in Opinion that such Statements furnish Ground for further Enquiry, they may require Schedules of the Parties' Property; and shall proceed to enquire into their Income: They may disclose such Schedules to the Affistants, and examine other Persons on Oath with like Powers as Commission--

XCVIII. And be it further enacted, That on the Day or Days fixed for taking any such Statements into Consideration, or on any Day to be previously named by them for that Purpose, the said respective Commercial Commissioners shall call to their Assistance any such Two or more Persons herein-after directed to be appointed for that Purpose, for the District of the said Commissioners, who in the Opinion of the said Commissioners may be, of those so appointed, best able to judge of the Amount of the reputed Income of the Person or Persons, Bodies, Corporations, Companies, Fraternities, or Societies, whose Statements shall be under Consideration before the said Commissioners, and shall enquire of such Persons their Opinion of such Amounts of reputed Income, or so much thereof as may arise from Trade or Manufacture, without disclosing to them, or any or either of them, the Amount contained in any Statement of such Person or Persons, Bodies, Corporations, Companies, Fraternities, or Societies; and if any or either of such Persons shall, upon such Inquiry, state the reputed Income of such Person or Persons, Bodies, Corporations, Companies, Fraternities, or Societies, at a Sum or Sums higher than, by Reference to the Statements delivered, the said Commissioners shall find the Sums contained therein respectively to be, then, unless Two Thirds or a greater Proportion of the said Commissioners shall concur in Opinion

sion that such Difference of Statement does ers in other Cases. not furnish sufficient Ground for further Inquiry, it shall be lawful for the said Commercial Commissioners, and they are hereby required, to issue their Precepts, requiring the Person or Persons, Bodies, Corporations, Companies, Fraternities, or Societies, delivering such Statements respectively, to return Schedules of their Property from which such Income may arise to the said Commissioners; which Schedules shall be made in the Manner and in the Form herein-before directed: And the said Commercial Commissioners shall, after issuing such Precepts, proceed to enquire into the Income arising from the Property stated in such Schedule, or any other Property belonging to such Person or Persons, Bodies, Corporations, Companies, Fraternities, or Societies, and shall be at Liberty to disclose the Particulars contained in such Schedule to the Assistants whom the said Commissioners shall have called in as aforesaid; and shall enquire from them, and shall also examine any other Person or Persons relative thereto, whom they may think necessary (upon Oath or solemn Affirmation, except as to such Assistants), in such Manner and Form and with the like Powers as the Commissioners for the Purposes of this Act are hereby authorized or enabled to do as before directed: And all Powers, Directions, Clauses, Matters, and Things, which are herein-before prescribed for the Conduct and Demeanour of the Commissioners for

the

the Purposes of this Act, except as herein-after is otherwise provided, shall be in full Force, and shall be practised and applied by the respective Commercial Commissioners, as fully and effectually as if the same Powers, Directions, Clauses, Matters, and Things, had been so expresly and particularly applied : Provided always, That the respective Persons to be examined before the said Commissioners shall be examined by them apart; and that the Evidence which they or any of them shall give shall not be disclosed to any Person or Persons whatever, except to such Assistants as aforesaid, for the Purpose of enabling them to form a Judgement of the actual Income then under Consideration as aforesaid.

Witnesses to be examined apart, and their Evidence not to be disclosed but to the Assistants.

XCIX. And be it further enacted, That after such Inquiry made by the said Commercial Commissioners as aforesaid, or any Three or more of them, it shall be lawful for the said Commissioners before whom such Inquiry shall have been made, or the major Part of them, and they are hereby required, according to the best of their Judgement, to settle and ascertain in what Sums such Person or Persons, Bodies, Corporations, Companies, Fraternities, or Societies, ought to be charged by virtue of this Act, and to make an Assessment or Assessments accordingly; and that when and as soon as the Amounts thereof shall be ascertained, the respective Commissioners of each such Com-

After such Enquiry, the Commercial Commissioners may proceed to ascertain the Assessment on the Parties, and each Committee [See § 97] shall enter the same in a Book to be kept privately by them, with the Name of the Party to be numbered or lettered progressively : Such Assess-

mittee

mittee ſhall cauſe the ſame to be entered in a Book to be by them reſpectively and privately kept, as herein-after mentioned, with the Name or Names, or Deſcription of the Perſon or Perſons, Bodies, Corporations, Companies, Fraternities, or Societies to be charged therewith, ſet oppoſite thereto; and which Entries ſhall be reſpectively numbered progreſſively, or lettered or diſtinguiſhed by Numbers and Letters, as the ſaid reſpective Commercial Commiſſioners ſhall think proper; and which Aſſeſſments, ſo made and entered, ſhall be final and concluſive to all Intents and Purpoſes whatever without Appeal: And that when and as ſoon as the ſaid reſpective Commiſſioners ſhall have cauſed to be made any ſuch Entry in ſuch Book, they ſhall deliver to the Perſon or Perſons, Bodies, Corporations, Companies, Fraternities, or Societies, charged by ſuch Aſſeſſments, or to ſome Perſon or Perſons there attending on his, her, or their Behalf, a Certificate or Certificates under the Hands and Seals of Two or more of ſuch Commiſſioners, ſpecifying the Amount of the Sums to be paid upon every ſuch Aſſeſſment reſpectively, to be reſpectively marked and numbered, or lettered, with the ſame Number or Letter as the Entry or Entries in the private Book of the ſaid Commiſſioners, to which ſuch Certificate or Certificates ſhall reſpectively relate, ſhall be marked and numbered or lettered, and which Certificates ſhall be cut off indentwiſe from the Counterparts thereof, which

ment to be final without Appeal. After ſuch Entry, a Duplicate of a Certificate ſhall be delivered to the Party under the Hands of Two Commiſſioners, ſtating the Amount of the Aſſeſſment, and its correſponding Number or Letter.

G 3 ſhall

shall also contain the like Sums, and be marked and numbered or lettered in the same Manner as the Certificate or Certificates to be so delivered as aforesaid; which Certificates, marked and numbered or lettered as aforesaid, containing the Amount of the said Assessments as aforesaid, without naming or describing the Person or Persons, Bodies, Corporations, Companies, Fraternities, or Societies, charged thereby, shall, on Production thereof, be a sufficient Authority to the Governor and Company of the Bank of *England*, and to the respective Receivers General and their respective Deputies in *England*, and to the Receiver General in *Scotland*, from Time to Time, to receive from any Person or Persons bearing and producing such Certificate or Certificates, the Amount of the Sums therein respectively contained, in such Proportions thereof as by this Act are made payable by Instalments, and at the Times by this Act appointed for Payment thereof, in Discharge and Satisfaction of the Assessment made by the said Commissioners for the last mentioned Purposes, and entered by them under the Letter or Number marked on such Certificate; and upon the Payment of such Sums contained in any such Certificate, or any Proportion thereof as aforesaid, to give Certificates for the same, acknowledging the Receipt of the Sum paid on Account of the Certificate of the said respective Commissioners, by the Number or Letter marked thereon as before directed.

C. And

C. And be it further enacted, That if in the Course of any Inquiry before the said Commercial Commissioners, they shall think it necessary to ascertain the Income of any Person or Persons, Bodies, Corporations, Companies, Fraternities, or Societies, who shall have delivered to them any such Statement or Statements as aforesaid, which Income, or any Part thereof, shall arise from any Property in *Great Britain* not engaged in Trade or Manufacture, out of the Limits of the City, Town, or Place, or its Vicinity, for which they shall act, the Commissioners for the Affairs of Taxes shall, on a Certificate or Certificates thereof, transmit such Certificates to the respective Commissioners for the Purposes of this Act, acting for the Division or Place, or Divisions or Places, where such Property, or any Part thereof, is or shall be situate; and the said last mentioned Commissioners shall, on Receipt of such Certificates, respectively enquire into the Amount of the Income arising from such Property within the Limits of the Division or Place where such last mentioned Commissioners act, and in proceeding therein it shall be lawful for them to use and apply all the Powers contained in this Act, in the same Manner as if such Person or Persons, Bodies, Corporations, Companies, Fraternities, or Societies, were chargeable under this Act in such Division or Place; and the said Commissioners, having satisfied themselves of such Income, shall, without allowing any Deduc-

If, in the Course of their Enquiries, Commercial Commissioners shall think it necessary to ascertain the Income of the Parties, any Part of which shall arise from Property in Great Britain, not in Trade, out of the Limits of the Jurisdiction of such Commissioners, the Tax Office shall transmit a Certificate from such Commissioners to the Commissioners of any other Division, to enquire into the Party's Income there; which they shall accordingly do, and certify the same to the Tax Office, to be laid before the Commercial Commissioners, to enable them to assess the Party; such last mentioned Certificate to be final and conclusive as

tion

to the Amount of Income contained therein.

tion to be made therefrom, (other than the special Deductions authorized by this Act in respect of such Property), transmit a Certificate thereof, under the Hands of any Two or more of them, to the said Commissioners for the Affairs of Taxes, to be laid before the said Commercial Commissioners, to the End that such Person or Persons, Bodies, Corporations, Companies, Fraternities, or Societies, may be justly charged upon the whole of his, her, or their Income; and such Certificates of the Commissioners for the Purposes of this Act shall be final and conclusive as to the Amount of Income contained therein, all just Deductions (other than the special Deductions aforesaid) being first made therefrom by the Commercial Commissioners, in the same Manner as if such Income had been ascertained by them in the First Instance.

Persons whose Income is under Enquiry before Commercial Commissioners, may apply for and obtain such Certificates, in order to have an Allowance on their whole Income.

CI. And be it further enacted, That if any Person, whose Income shall be under Inquiry before the Commercial Commissioners, shall apply to them to ascertain, in Manner before directed, the Amount of any Income arising from Property not subject to Inquiry before such Commercial Commissioners, in order to have any Allowance made from the Whole of his or her Income, it shall be lawful for them, and they are hereby required to deliver the proper Certificate for that Purpose; which Certificate shall be carried into Effect in the Manner before directed: And the said Commercial

mercial Commiffioners, after having received the Account of fuch Income, fhall, in order to make any Allowances to which fuch Perfon may be entitled in refpect of the Whole of his or her Income, add the fame to the Amount of Income afcertained by fuch Commercial Commiffioners, and therefrom make fuch Allowances accordingly.

CII. And be it further enacted, That any Income arifing from Property in any of the British Plantations in America, and imported into Great Britain from thence, may be ftated, proved, afcertained, and affeffed to, before and by the refpective Commercial Commiffioners acting for the refpective Places herein-after mentioned, videlicet, London, Briftol, Liverpool, and Glasgow, in the fame Manner as if fuch Income had arifen from Trade or Manufacture carried on in fuch Places refpectively: And fuch Income fhall be affeffed and charged by the Commiffioners acting for fuch of the faid Places at or neareft to which fuch Property fhall have been firft imported into Great Britain.

Income from Property in the American Plantations may be afcertained by the Commercial Commiffioners for London, Briftol, Liverpool, or Glasgow; and be affeffed by the Commiffioners of either of thofe Places neareft to which the Property is firft imported hither.

CIII. And be it further enacted, That any Income received in Great Britain, and arifing from Property of any Perfon or Perfons in fuch Plantations as aforefaid, which fhall not have been imported into Great Britain, may be ftated, proved, afcertained, and affeffed, in like Manner as aforefaid, together with the Income of the fame Perfon

Income received in Great Britain arifing from Property of Perfons in fuch Plantations not imported here, may be alfo afcertained in like Manner.

or

or Perfons arifing from fuch Property which
fhall have been imported as aforefaid, in
cafe any fuch Income arifing from Property
imported as aforefaid fhall be ftated to fuch
Commercial Commiffioners, in order to be
affeffed and charged under this Act.

One Committee of Commercial Commiffioners [fee § 97] may affefs the Members of another Committee, with Power of Appeal to all fuch Commiffioners; but the Parties interefted fhall have no Vote.

CIV. And be it further enacted, That in
every Place where the Number of Commercial Commiffioners to be appointed as aforefaid fhall be fufficient to divide themfelves
into Two or more Committees as aforefaid,
it fhall be lawful for the Perfons compofing
any one fuch Committee to affefs and
charge the Perfons compofing any other fuch
Committee until each fuch Commiffioner
fhall be fully affeffed and charged, with
Power of Appeal to all the faid Commiffioners; and that where fuch Committees
fhall be formed, the faid Commiffioners fhall
eftablifh fuch Regulations amongft themfelves
for affeffing and charging each other, as may
moft effectually fecure a fair and impartial
Affeffment upon every fuch Commiffioner,
according to the true Intent and Meaning of
this Act: Provided that upon any fuch
Appeal the Commiffioner interefted fhall
have no Voice, but fhall withdraw until the
Determination thereof, in the Manner hereinbefore directed with refpect to Commiffioners for the Purpofes of this Act.

§ 70.

Where fuch Commiffioners are not

CV. And be it further enacted, That
where the faid Commiffioners fhall not be
fufficient

fufficient to divide themfelves into Committees as aforefaid, every fuch Commiffioner fhall be affeffed and charged by the other Commiffioners prefent; in which Cafe the Commiffioner interefted fhall have no Voice; but fhall withdraw until the Determination thereof in Manner before directed: Provided that if any fuch Commiffioner fhall think himfelf aggrieved by the Determination of the other Commiffioners as aforefaid, it fhall be lawful for him to appeal to the Commercial Commiffioners acting for the City of London, who fhall hear and determine the fame, and affefs and charge fuch Appellant under the like Powers, and fubject to the like Rules, as they might have affeffed and charged fuch Appellant in cafe he had refided within the City of London, and had in the Firft Inftance delivered to the faid Commercial Commiffioners his Statement for that Purpofe.

[marginal note: divided into Committees, each Commiffioner fhall be affeffed by the others, with Appeal to the Commercial Commiffioners for London.]

CVI. And be it further enacted, That the Commercial Commiffioners acting within and for the City of London and its Vicinity, comprehending the Diftrict herein-after defcribed, fhall, on or before the Fifth Day of June yearly, during the Term herein mentioned, or as foon after as can be conveniently done, tranfmit the Counterparts of all fuch Certificates as fhall have been iffued by them to the Cafhier of the Governor and Company of the Bank of England, in order that all Perfons, Bodies, Corporations, Companies,

[marginal note: The Commercial Commiffioners for London and its Vicinity [fee § 110] fhall, yearly, before June 5, or as foon as poffible after, tranfmit to the Bank the Counterparts of all Certificates iffued by them, that the Parties may pay their Affeffments]

there, and the Commercial Commiffioners for other Cities and Diftricts, [*see* § 111, 112], shall tanfmit fuch Counterparts to the refpective Receivers General; and the Bank and Receivers General fhall open Accounts with fuch Commercial Commiffioners as to all Money received on fuch Certificates.

panies, Fraternities, and Societies, affeffed by the faid Commiffioners, may pay, in Manner before directed, their Affeffments into the faid Bank of *England:* And the refpective Commercial Commiffioners acting within or for any City, Town, or Place herein-after mentioned, or any other City, Town, or Place, in *Great Britain*, for which, and their refpective Vicinities, Commiffioners for the faid laft mentioned Purpofes fhall be appointed according to the Directions of this Act, fhall within the like Period, tranfmit the Counterparts of all fuch Certificates, as fhall have been iffued by them refpectively in *England*, to the Receiver General of the County, Riding, or Place where fuch Certificates have been iffued, or their refpective Deputies, and in *Scotland* to the Receiver General there: And the Cafhier of the faid Bank of *England*, and the refpective Receivers General, or their refpective Deputies as aforefaid, fhall, upon the Receipt of any Sum of Money on Account of any fuch Certificate, figned and marked, and numbered or lettered as aforefaid, enter the fame in a Book to be provided for that Purpofe, with the Number and Figure marked in fuch Certificate fet oppofite thereto, under the Head of " The Account of the Commercial " Commiffioners acting for the " of   and its Vicinity."

The refpective Commercial Commiffion-

CVII. And be it further enacted, That the faid refpective Commercial Commiffion-

ers

ers shall from Time to Time transmit to the Commissioners for the Affairs of Taxes, the gross Amount of all Assessments made by them up to the Day of making up such Account; and that when and as soon as such Assessments shall be completed in any such District, the said respective Commissioners acting therein shall cause to be delivered a Schedule or Duplicate on Parchment, under their Hands and Seals, fairly written, containing the whole Sum assessed by the said Commissioners, unto the said respective Receivers General, and shall transmit, or cause to be transmitted, a like Schedule or Duplicate into the King's Remembrancer's Office of the Exchequer in *England* and *Scotland* respectively.

ers shall, from Time to Time, transmit to the Tax Office, Accounts of the Gross Amount of their Assessments; and when such Assessments are compleated, shall deliver a Schedule of the whole Amount to the Receivers General, and transmit a Duplicate thereof into the Exchequer.

CVIII. And be it further enacted, That all Books, Papers, and Writings whatever, belonging to or provided by the said Commercial Commissioners, shall be carefully preserved and kept in their Custody, or of some or One of them, or in such Manner as they shall think confistent with the Secrecy to be observed in the Custody thereof.

All such Commissioners Books, etc. shall be kept in their Custody, or as they shall think most confistent with Secrecy.

CIX. And be it further enacted, That the Cashier of the Bank of *England*, and the respective Receivers General, shall, Ten Days before the Second, and so before every subsequent Instalment, transmit to the respective Commercial Commissioners as aforesaid, a true Account of all Sums paid on
Account

Ten Days before each Instalment, the Bank and Receivers General shall transmit to the respective Commercial Commissioners, an Account of

Sums paid, and remaining unpaid, on prior Inftalments, and the Numbers, *etc.* to which they relate; and fuch Commiffioners fhall give Notice to the Party concerned, to pay all Arrears within a certain Time; and on Failure of Payment, may iffue their Warrant for levying the fame.

Account of any prior Inftalment or Inftalments, and alfo of any Sum or Sums which may remain unpaid on Account of fuch prior Inftalment or Inftalments, and the refpective Numbers and Letters to which fuch Sums fo remaining unpaid fhall refpectively relate: And the faid refpective Commiffioners fhall, upon Reference to their private Books, by Notice in Writing under the Hands of any Two of them, to be tranfmitted to the Perfon or Perfons, or the Chamberlain, Treafurer, Cafhier, or other Officer aforefaid, of any Body, Corporation, Company, Fraternity, or Society, making fuch Default, require him, her, or them, to pay the Sum fo in Arrear within a Time to be fixed, in fuch Notice: And if any Perfon or Perfons fo charged, or if the Chamberlain, Treafurer, Cafhier, or other Officer aforefaid, of any Body, Corporation, Company, Fraternity, or Society, fo charged, fhall neglect to pay the fame within the Time limited in fuch Notice, it fhall be lawful for the faid refpective Commercial Commiffioners for the laft mentioned Purpofes, and they are hereby required to iffue their Warrant for the levying the Sum and Sums fo in Arrear and unpaid, in fuch Manner, and to fuch Effect and Purpofe, as any other of the Commiffioners before mentioned for the Purpofes of this Act may, under this Act, or the Commiffioners appointed to carry into Execution any of the faid Acts herein-before referred to, may, under the faid Acts, levy any

Money

Money due to His Majefty, His Heirs or Succeffors, of the Rates and Duties charged and levied under this Act, or the faid Acts fo referred to, or any of them.

CX. And be it further enacted, That within and for the City of *London* and its Vicinity, as herein-after mentioned, *videlicet,* the City and Liberty of *Weftminfter,* the Borough of *Southwark,* the feveral Parifhes within the Bills of Mortality, and the Parifhes of *Saint Mary-le-Bone* and *Saint Pancras,* and all Parifhes within the Counties of *Middlefex, Effex, Kent,* and *Surrey,* any Part whereof fhall be fituate within Ten Miles of the *Royal Exchange,* there fhall be appointed Twenty-four Perfons, qualified as herein-after is required, who fhall be Commercial Commiffioners within the faid Diftrict, or fuch other lefs Number as can be found therein fo qualified, to afcertain the Income of Perfons engaged in Trade and Manufacture refident within the faid Diftrict, and of all fuch Bodies Politick and Corporate (except Corporation Sole refiding without the faid Diftrict), Companies, Fraternities, and Societies of Perfons in *Great Britain,* who fhall be defirous of being affeffed under the faid Commiffioners ; and alfo Twenty-four other Perfons, in like Manner qualified, or fuch lefs Number as may be found therein fo qualified, to act in the Affiftance of the faid Commercial Commiffioners: And that Three of the Perfons

For the City of *London,* and its Vicinity, (including *Weftminfter, Southwark,* the Bills of Mortality, *Mary-le-bone, Pancras,* and every Parifh in *Middlefex, Effex, Kent,* and *Surrey,* any Part of which is within 10 Miles of the *Royal Exchange*), 24 Perfons fhall be appointed, (qualified as in § 114) to be Commercial Commiffioners for fuch Diftrict, and 24 others as Affiftants. Three fuch Commiffioners, and Three fuch Affiftants, to be named by the Mayor and Aldermen, out of 12, (Six being Aldermen), to be returned by the Common.

10

Council; Three by the Bank, Three by the *East India* Company, Three by the *South Sea* Company, Two by each of the Two Insurance Companies, and Two by the Grand Jurors of each of the said FourCounties.

so to be appointed Commissioners, and Three of the said Assistants, shall be named by the Mayor and Aldermen of *London*, out of Twelve Persons, Six of whom shall be Aldermen, to be returned to them by the Common Council as aforesaid : Three other Commissioners and Three other Assistants by the Governors and Directors of the Bank of *England* : Three other Commissioners and Three other Assistants by the Directors of the said United Company trading to the *East Indies* : Three other Commissioners and Three other Assistants by the Governors aforesaid and Directors of the *South Sea* Company : Two other Commissioners and Two other Assistants by each of the respective Governors and Directors of the several Insurance Companies before mentioned : And Two other Commissioners and Two other Assistants by each of the Grand Inquests as aforesaid, having been returned to serve for the several Counties of *Middlesex*, *Essex*, *Kent*, and *Surrey*, as before mentioned.

For *Birmingham, Liverpool, Leeds, Manchester, King's Lynn,* and *Glasgow,* and for such other Cities, *etc.* as the respective Persons, empowered to nominate Commissioners,

CXI. And be it further enacted, That, within and for the several Towns and Places herein-after mentioned, *videlicet,* *Birmingham,* *Liverpool, Leeds, Manchester, King's Lynn,* and *Glasgow,* and such Cities and other Towns and Places in *Great Britain,* (Regard being had to the Extent of Trade and Manufacture thereof), as the Persons who are respectively empowered to nominate Commissioners for the Purposes of this Act,

for

for the County, Riding, Shire, or Stewartry at large within which such Place shall be situate, shall think proper to name Commercial Commissioners to act therein for such Purposes as aforesaid, there shall be appointed by the said Persons so empowered, so many Persons, qualified as herein is required, to be Commercial Commissioners within and for such Cities, Towns, and Places respectively, and within and for such Parishes and Places in the Vicinity of such Cities, Towns, and Places respectively, as the respective Inquests before-mentioned shall think proper to be included in the same Districts with such Cities, Towns, and Places respectively: And the said last mentioned Persons to be appointed as aforesaid, shall be Commissioners to ascertain the Income of Persons engaged in Trade and Manufacture resident within the said respective Districts, and of all such Bodies Politick and Corporate, Companies, and Societies of Persons in such Districts respectively, who shall be desirous of being assessed under the said Commissioners respectively: And in every such District there shall also be appointed so many Persons, qualified as herein is required, to act as Assistants to the said respective Commercial Commissioners within their Districts: Provided that the Number of Commissioners to be appointed for each such District as aforesaid, shall not be less than Three nor more than Twelve; and that the Assistants to be also appointed for each such Dis-

shall think proper, Commercial Commissioners, and Assistants shall be appointed by such Inquest, to act for such Towns and certain Districts in the Vicinity of each; not less than Three, nor more than Twelve Commissioners for each District.

H trict

trict shall not be less than Three nor more than Twelve.

For *Bristol, Exeter, Hull, Newcastle upon Tyne, Norwich,* and *Edinburgh,* and such other Cities being Counties of themselves, as such Inquests shall think fit, (with their Vicinities), Commercial Commissioners shall be appointed by the acting Magistrates of the said Cities, etc.

CXII. Provided always, and be it further enacted, That within and for the several Cities, Towns, and Places herein-after mentioned, videlicet, *Bristol, Exeter, Hull, Newcastle-upon-Tyne, Norwich,* and *Edinburgh,* and also such other Cities, Towns, and Places, in *Great Britain,* being respectively Counties of themselves, for which the said Jurors for the respective Counties at large as aforesaid shall think proper that Commercial Commissioners should be named, there shall be appointed by the respective Persons acting as Magistrates or Justices of the Peace for such Cities, Towns, and Places respectively, being Counties of themselves as aforesaid, so many Persons qualified as herein is required to be Commercial Commissioners within and for such Cities, Towns, and Places respectively, and within and for such Parishes and Places in the Vicinity of such Cities, Towns, and Places respectively, as the respective Inquests for the Counties at large before mentioned shall think proper to be included in the same Districts with such Cities, Towns, and Places respectively: And the said last mentioned Commissioners, after their Appointment by the respective Magistrates and Justices of the Peace of the Cities, Towns, and Places, being Counties of themselves as aforesaid, shall have and exercise the like Powers, and in as ample a Manner as if they had been respectively
tively

tively appointed by the respective Inquests of the Counties at large.

CXIII. Provided always, and be it further enacted, That any Person or Persons engaged in any Trade or Manufacture, and residing in the County, Riding, Shire, or Stewartry where any such Commercial Commissioner shall be appointed, (in case any such Commissioners shall be so appointed in such County or Riding,) although not resident within the District of the Commercial Commissioners, shall and may be charged to the Rates and Duties granted by this Act by such Commercial Commissioner's, if such Person or Persons shall prefer such Charge, and pursue the Rules and Regulations hereinbefore prescribed for causing such Charge to be made: And in case no such Commercial Commissioners shall be so appointed in the County, Riding, Shire, or Stewartry, where such Person or Persons shall reside, then such Person or Persons may apply in like Manner to the Commissioners for the Purposes of this Act, for the Division or Place where such Person or Persons shall reside: And the respective Commissioners for the Purposes of this Act shall in any such Case require the Assistance of any Two or more Persons whose Names shall be inserted in the List made out by the Jurors upon the Grand Inquest of the County, Riding, Shire, or Stewartry where such Division or Place shall be situate; and shall, in ascertaining

Any Trader residing in the County where such Commercial Commissioners are appointed (though not resident within their District) may elect to be assessed by them; or (in case no such Commissioners are appointed in that County) then by the other Commissioners under this Act, assisted by Two Persons from the Grand Jurors List, who shall then act as Commercial Commissioners.

H 2 the

the Charge to be made upon such Person or Persons, pursue all such Rules, Directions, and Regulations, and shall have such Powers as are herein-before prescribed and given for the Conduct of Commercial Commissioners especially appointed under this Act as aforesaid; and the Sum so charged shall be paid and accounted for in the same Manner.

Commercial Commissioners shall be qualified as other Commissioners under this Act for a County at large: [See § 23:] Acting without such Qualification, to forfeit 100l.

CXIV. Provided always, and be it further enacted, That no Person shall be capable of acting as a Commercial Commissioner under this Act, or as an Assistant to such Commissioners, who shall not be seised or possessed of an Estate of the like Nature and Value as is herein-before required for a Commissioner for the Purposes of this Act as aforesaid, for a County at large: And if any Person, not qualified as aforesaid, shall act in the Execution of this Act as a Commercial Commissioner, every such Person shall forfeit the Sum of One hundred Pounds, to be recovered as any Penalty may be recovered by the said first recited Act.

Commercial Commissioners' Oath to be the same as that of other Commissioners, and subscribed, &c. (according to § 22.)

CXV. And be it further enacted, That every Person to be appointed a Commercial Commissioner as aforesaid, before he shall begin to act therein, (except in administering the Oath herein referred to), shall take the same Oath as is herein-before required to be taken by a Commissioner for the Purposes of this Act; which Oath so taken shall be subscribed, and the Names of the Persons taking
ing

ing the fame fhall be tranfmitted in the Manner before directed with refpect to the Commiffioners for the Purpofes of this Act.

CXVI, And be it further enacted, That every Perfon to be appointed an Affiftant to the Commercial Commiffioners, fhall before the faid Commiffioners take the following Oath; (that is to fay), *Affiftants to Commiffioners to take the following*

' I *A. B.* do fwear, That in the Execution *Oath.*
' of an Act, [*Here fet forth the Title of*
' *this Act*], I will in all Refpects act fairly,
' honeftly, and impartially, and without Fa-
' vour, Affection, or Malice, to the beft of
' my Knowledge and Belief: And that I will
' not difclofe any Particular contained in any
' Schedule of Income of any Perfon, Body
' Politick or Corporate, Company, Frater-
' nity, or Society of Perfons whatever, which
' fhall be fhewn to me in the Execution of
' the faid Act, except in fuch Cafes only
' where it fhall be neceffary to difclofe the
' fame for the Purpofes of the faid Act, or
' in order to or in the Courfe of a Profecu-
' tion for Perjury committed in any Matter
' relating to fuch Schedule.
　　　　　' So help me GOD,'

CXVII. And be it further enacted, That the faid refpective Commercial Commiffioners fhall and may appoint and employ a Clerk, and fuch other Officer or Officers as may be neceffary, with the Confent and Approbation *Commercial Commiffioners may employ a Clerk, who fhall take an Oath of Fidelity, and alfo the Oath*
　　　　　　　H 3　　　　　　　　　　of

of the Commissioners of the Treasury, or any Three of them, and shall and may give and administer to such Clerk, and other Officer or Officers respectively, an Oath for their faithful Demeanor in all Things relating to the due Performance of the Trusts reposed in them by the said respective Commercial Commissioners, and also the Oath herein-before required to be taken by Clerks to the respective Commissioners for the Purposes of this Act; which Oaths shall be duly subscribed by the Parties taking the same: And the said respective Commercial Commissioners shall and may, from Time to Time, at their Discretion, dismiss and discharge such Clerk, or other Officer or Officers, and appoint others in their Place: And the said Clerks and other Officers are hereby required faithfully to execute and perform the said Trusts in them respectively reposed, without taking any Thing for such Service, other than such Salaries or Rewards as the said respective Commercial Commissioners, with the Consent and Approbation of the Commissioners of the Treasury, or any Three or more of them, shall allow, in Manner herein-after directed.

CXVIII. And be it further enacted, That the Commissioners of the Treasury, or any Three or more of them, for the Time being, are hereby respectively authorized, from Time to Time, to direct the Cashier or Cashiers of the Bank of *England*, or the respective

tive Receivers General before-mentioned, as may be most convenient, to advance and pay, out of the Monies arising from the said Rates and Duties granted by this Act, to such Person or Persons as the said respective Commercial Commissioners, or the major Part of them acting for any District as aforesaid, shall respectively name, such Sums of Money as shall appear to the said Commissioners of the Treasury necessary for the last mentioned Purposes of this Act; which Sums so to be advanced shall be applied for the Payment of Allowances, and in defraying all other necessary Charges and Expences in or about the Execution of this Act, in respect to the Commercial Commissioners, without other Account than before the Lords Commissioners of His Majesty's Treasury.

CXIX. And be it further enacted, That all the Monies arising by the said Rates and Duties, (the necessary Charges of raising and accounting for the same excepted), and also all Monies to be received at the Bank of *England* under this Act, shall from Time to Time be paid into the Receipt of His Majesty's Exchequer, distinctly and apart from all other Branches of the Publick Revenues; and that there shall be provided and kept in the Office of the Auditor of the said Receipt of Exchequer, a Book or Books, in which all the Monies arising from the said respective Rates and Duties, or received at the Bank of *England*, and paid into the said Receipt as aforesaid,

The Money raised under this Act shall be paid into the Exchequer, and the Account thereof kept distinct.

said, shall be entered separate and apart from all other Monies paid or payable to His Majesty, His Heirs and Successors, upon any Account whatever: And the said Monies, so paid into the said Receipt, shall be subject and liable to the Uses and Purposes hereinafter mentioned.

Recital of the Application of the Duties under 38 *Geo.* 3. *c.* 16 (§ 97) and of the Duties under 38 *Geo.* 3. *c.* 76 (§ 38.)

CXX. And whereas all the Monies arising from the Additional Rates and Assessments, or from Payments at the Bank of *England,* by virtue of the said recited Act of the last Session of Parliament, intituled, *An Act for granting to His Majesty an Aid and Contribution for the Prosecution of the War,* together with the Duties granted by another Act of the last Session of Parliament, intituled, *An Act for the better Protection of the Trade of this Kingdom, and for granting new and additional Duties of Customs on Goods imported and exported, and on the Tonnage of certain Ships entering outwards or inwards to or from Foreign Parts, until the signing the Preliminary Articles of Peace,* not exceeding in the Whole the Sum of Seven Millions, which should be paid into the said Receipt of the Exchequer, were, from Time to Time, as the same should be paid into the said Receipt, directed to be issued and applied to such Services as are in the said first recited Act mentioned: Be

All Money raised under those Acts, and also under this Act, not exceeding Se-

it further enacted, That all the Monies arising from the said Rates and Assessments by the said recited Acts granted, or from Payments at the Bank of *England,* and also from
the

the Rates and Duties hereby granted, not exceeding the said Sum of Seven Millions, which shall be paid into the said Receipt of the Exchequer, shall from Time to Time, as the same shall be paid into the said Receipt, be issued and applied either to the Services voted by the Commons of *Great Britain*, in the said last Session of Parliament, for the Service of the Year One thousand seven hundred and ninety-eight; or to the Payment and Discharge of all Annuities, Interest, and Dividends, which have or shall become payable in consequence of the Loan of Eight Millions raised by virtue of another Act passed in the said last Session of Parliament: And that, after issuing or reserving at the said Receipt of Exchequer, out of the said Monies, such Sums as shall be sufficient for the Purposes aforesaid, the Surplus of the said Monies, as the same shall arise and be paid into the said Receipt, shall be and are hereby appropriated for the Services which shall then have been voted by the Commons of *Great Britain* for the Service of the Year One thousand seven hundred and ninety-nine, or shall be voted by the said Commons for the Service of any subsequent Year, not exceeding Ten Millions in any one Year, and which shall be specifically charged on the said Rates and Duties by any Act or Acts to be passed for that Purpose; and in the next Place for the Payment and Discharge of all Annuities, Interest, and Dividends, which shall become payable in

consequence

[margin:] ven Millions, shall be applied to the Services of the Year 1798; or in paying the Interest of the Loan of Eight Millions raised last Session: The Surplus to be appropriated to the Services of the Year 1799, or of any subsequent Year, specifically charged on the said Duties, not exceeding 10 Millions in any One Year; next in Payment of the Interest of any Loans to be specifically charged thereon; and lastly, in the Purchase of Stock to the Amount of the Stock created by such Loans: The Money to be issued and applied accordingly.

confequence of any Loan or Loans, which
fhall alfo be fpecifically charged on the faid
Rates and Duties by fuch Act or Acts; and
laftly, for the Purchafe of Publick Annuities to the Amount of the Annuities
which may be created on fuch Loan or
Loans: And the Commiffioners of His
Majefty's Treafury now or for the Time
being, or any Three or more of them, or the
High Treafurer for the Time being, are or
is hereby authorized and required to iffue
and apply the fame for the Services of each
Year fucceffively, to fuch Amount yearly
as fhall have been then voted by the Commons of *Great Britain*, not exceeding Ten
Millions in any One Year; and in the next
Place to the Payment and Difcharge of the
Annuities, Intereft, and Dividends which
fhall become payable in confequence of fuch
Loan or Loans, as and when the fame fhall
become payable: And that, after applying
fuch Part of the faid Monies as fhall be fufficient for the Services of each Year fucceffively as aforefaid, and for the Payment
and Difcharge of all fuch Annuities, Dividends, and Intereft as aforefaid, or referving
the fame at the faid Receipt of Exchequer,
the Commiffioners of His Majefty's Treafury for the Time being, or any Three or
more of them, or the Lord High Treafurer
for the Time being, are or is hereby authorized and required to iffue, from Time to
Time, the Surplus of the faid Monies arifing
from the Rates and Duties by this Act granted,

ed, during the Term for which the said Rates and Duties are hereby granted, to the Governor and Company of the Bank of *England*, to be placed to the Account of the Commissioners appointed by an Act, passed in the Twenty-sixth Year of the Reign of His present Majesty, for applying certain Sums annually to the Reduction of the National Debt; who shall apply the same in Payment for the Purchase of any Publick Annuities, in the Manner directed by the said recited Act, passed in the Thirty-eighth Year of the Reign of His present Majesty, for granting an Aid and Contribution for the Prosecution of the War, so long as the same shall be so applicable under and by virtue of this Act.

c. 16. § 98, 99, 100.

CXXI. And be it further enacted, That upon the Purchase by the said Commissioners appointed for the Reduction of the National Debt, out of the Monies to arise as aforesaid, of Publick Annuities to the Amount of all the Annuities which may be created on any Loan or Loans specifically to be charged on the said Rates and Duties as aforesaid, the said Rates and Duties shall be determined in the Manner directed by the said last mentioned Act; and all the Powers, Provisions, and Rules, contained in the said last mentioned Act, for issuing and applying the Monies arising from, and for determining, the Rates and Assessments granted thereby, shall severally and respectively be in full Force,

The Duties to cease, on the Purchase, by the Commissioners of the National Debt, of Stock to the Amount of Stock created by any Loans to be specifically charged on the said Duties; as under 38 Geo. III, c. 16, § 101, &c.

Force, and put in Practice, for the issuing and applying the Monies arising from, and for determining, at the Period herein mentioned, the Rates and Duties hereby granted, as fully and effectually as if the same had been repeated and re-enacted in this present Act.

Every Appeal decided on the Ground of Income, under 38 Geo. III, c. 16, shall be conclusive, except where the Party shall prove [under § 71 of that Act] that his Income for the Year ending Feb. 5, fell short of the Sum declared, or was diminished from some specifick Cause; [See § 72 of that Act;] in which Cases the Commissioners of Appeal, under that Act, may give Relief.

CXXII. And be it further enacted, That every Appeal on the Ground of Income, once heard and determined, under and by virtue of the said Act, passed in the Thirty-eighth Year aforesaid, for granting an Aid and Contribution as aforesaid, shall be final and conclusive during the Continuance of the Rates and Duties granted by the said Act, as is herein-before limited; except where the Party shall alledge and prove, in the Manner directed by the said Act, that his or her Income, during the Year ending on the Fifth Day of *February* One thousand seven hundred and ninety-nine, fell short of the Sum mentioned in his or her Declaration by a stated Sum: In which Case; and also where the Income of any Person has been diminished from any specifick Cause arising after the Time allowed for hearing Appeals in the Year preceding the said Fifth Day of *February* One thousand seven hundred and ninety-nine; it shall be lawful for the respective Commissioners for hearing and determining Appeals under the said Act, to give Relief to the Appellant or Appellants in the Manner directed by the said Act.

CXXIII. And

CXXIII. Provided always, and be it further enacted, That it shall and may be lawful to and for any Justice of the Peace residing near the Place where the Offence shall be committed, to hear and determine any Offence against this Act, which subjects the Offender to any pecuniary Penalty not exceeding Twenty Pounds; which said Justice of the Peace is hereby authorized and required, upon any Information exhibited or Complaint made in that Behalf, within Three Calendar Months after the Offence committed, to summon the Party accused, giving to each Party Three Days Notice to appear, and also the Witnesses on either Side, and to examine into the Matter of Fact; and upon Proof made thereof, either by Voluntary Confession of the Party accused, or by the Oath of One or more credible Witness or Witnesses, or otherwise, as the Case may require, to give Judgement or Sentence for the Penalty or Forfeiture as in and by this Act is directed; to be divided, One Moiety thereof to the Poor of the Parish or Place where the Offence shall be committed, and the other Moiety thereof to the Informer or Informers; and to award and issue out his Warrant, under his Hand and Seal, for the levying the said Penalty adjudged, of the Goods of the Offender, and to cause Sale to be made thereof in case they shall not be redeemed within Six Days, rendering to the Party the Overplus (if any); and where the Goods of such Offender cannot be found sufficient to

answer

[Marginal note: Justices of Peace may determine Offences under this Act where the Penalty does not exceed 20l.; on Complaint within Three Months; Summoning the Party accused and Witnesses; and may convict on Confession of the Party, or Oath of One Witness: The Penalty to go Half to the Poor and Half to the Informer; to be levied by Distress and Sale, or on Default the Offender to suffer not more than Six, nor less than Three, Months' Imprisonment.]

answer the Penalty, to commit such Offender
to Prison, there to remain for any Space of
Time not exceeding Six nor lefs than Three
Calendar Months, unlefs such pecuniary Penalty shall be sooner paid and satisfied: And
if either Party shall find himself or themselves
aggrieved by the Judgement of any such
Justice, then he and they shall and may,
upon giving Security to the Amount of the
Value of such Penalty and Forfeiture, together
with such Costs as shall be awarded in cafe
such Judgement shall be affirmed, appeal to
the Justices of the Peace at the next General
Quarter Seffions for the County, Riding,
Division, Shire, Stewartry, or Place, which
shall happen after Fourteen Days next after
such Conviction shall have been made, (and
of which Appeal reasonable Notice shall
be given,) who are hereby empowered to
fummon and examine Witnesses upon Oath,
and finally to hear and determine the fame;
and in cafe the Judgement of such Justice
shall be affirmed, it shall be lawful for such
Justices to award the Person or Persons appealing to pay such Costs occasioned by such
Appeal, as to them shall feem meet: Provided neverthelefs, That it shall and may
be lawful to and for the said Justice, where
he shall see Caufe, to mitigate and leffen such
Penalties as he shall think fit, (reasonable
Costs and Charges of the Officers and Informers, as well in making the Difcovery
as in profecuting the fame, being always
allowed over and above such Mitigation),

and

Margin notes:

Appeal given
to the Quarter
Seffions who
may award
Costs.

Penalties may
be mitigated
to one Half,
over and
above the In-
former's Costs.

and fo as fuch Mitigation doth not reduce the Penalties to lefs than the Moiety of the Penalties incurred over and above the faid Cofts and Charges; any Thing contained in this Act to the contrary notwithftanding.

CXXIV. And be it further enacted, That this Act may be altered, varied, or repealed, by any Act or Acts to be made in this prefent Seffion of Parliament.

Act may be altered or repealed this Seffion.

SCHEDULE

SCHEDULE.

———

(A.)

RULES for eſtimating the Income to
ariſe within the current Year of
Perſons to be aſſeſſed under the Act
of the Thirty-ninth Year of the
Reign of His preſent Majeſty.

———

*I. INCOME ariſing from Lands, Tene-
ments, and Hereditaments.*

*General Rule for aſcertaining the Value of all
Lands.*

In all Caſes the Annual Value of Lands
ſhall be eſtimated from the Aggregate
Amount of the Rent at which the
ſame are let, or if not let, are worth
to be let by the Year, according to the
ordinary Rent of Lands of like Quality in the ſame Neighbourhood;
together with the Payments within
the Year for all Parochial and other
Taxes, Rates, and Aſſeſſments,
charged

charged upon the refpective Occupiers in refpect of fuch Lands; and alfo the Value of Tythes, where taken in Kind, or of the Sums paid in Satisfaction for the fame; after deducting from fuch Aggregate Amount the Fourth Part thereof.

1ft. *INCOME of Owners of Lands.*

FIRST CASE.

Income of Lands occupied by the Owner.

Such Income fhall be taken at the Amount of One Year's Rent, according to the Rate at which fuch Lands are worth to be let by the Year, according to the ordinary Rent of Lands of like Quality in the fame Neighbourhood, Regard being had to the Demands to which fuch Lands may be liable for or in refpect of Tythes, or any Satisfaction for the fame, or from which Demands fuch Lands may be free; and alfo a Sum not lefs than the Amount of One Quarter, or more than One Half, of the Annual Value, eftimated as aforefaid, in Addition to fuch Rent; and where the Lands have come into the Occupation of the Owner within Eighteen Months paft, on the Expiration of a Leafe, or the Death or Failure of a Tenant, then the fame fhall be valued at One Year's Rent only of Lands of the like Quality, eftimated as aforefaid.

I

DEDUCTIONS

DEDUCTIONS to be made from the FIRST
CASE.

The Amount of Land Tax payable from
the Fifth Day of *February* laft paft for One
Year.

The Amount of Fee Farm Rents, Quit,
Rents, Rent Charges, Ground Rents, and
other Rents payable by fuch Owner, or other
Charges which the Owner of the Land fhall
be bound by Tenure to pay, or for the Expence of Drainage under any Commiffion of
Sewers, eftimated for One Year, as aforefaid, next preceding the Delivery of the
Schedule.

Repairs of Buildings, confifting of a principal Meffuage, occupied by the Owner, and
other Buildings, occupied with a Farm of
Lands or Tythes at an Average, to be fettled
at the Difcretion of the Commiffioners under
all the Circumftances, not exceeding Eight
Pounds *per Centum* on the Annual Value of
the Farm, eftimated as aforefaid; but if there
be no principal Meffuage, then at the like
Average, not exceeding Three Pounds *per
Centum* on the like Annual Value:

Alfo on Account of Expences in draining
Lands, fuch Sum as the Commiffioners fhall
allow, not exceeding in any Cafe Three
Pounds *per Centum* on the Annual Value of
the Lands improved by fuch Drainage.

And in refpect of Embankments from the
Sea, or any River, when the fame fhall be
neceffary for the Occupation of Lands, or
by

by reason of Tenure therein, such Sum as the Commissioners, under all the Circumstances, shall allow.

SECOND CASE.

Houses and Buildings occupied by the Owner.

The Annual Value of such Houses or other Buildings shall be taken according to the fair Rent at which Houses of the like Description are usually let or might be let by the Year, unfurnished, as near as may be; but where the same are or shall be rated to the Tax on Inhabited Houses, then not to be taken at less than such Rate.

DEDUCTIONS.

Repairs, at the best Average, in the Judgement of the Commissioners, and not exceeding Ten Pounds *per Centum* on the Annual Value estimated as aforesaid.

Other Deductions as in the First Case.

THIRD CASE.

Lands in Occupation of Tenants at Rack Rent.

The Annual Value of such Lands shall be taken at the full Amount of the Rent reserved.

DEDUCTIONS.

As in the First Case, if payable by the Owner; and also the Amount of the Tythes,

I 2 or

or the Satisfaction for the fame, and Rates
and Taxes, if payable by the Owner, and
alfo the actual Expences of collecting the
Rents.

FOURTH CASE.

*Lands demifed to Tenants in Confideration of a
Fine paid and Rent referved.*

The Annual Value of fuch Lands fhall be
taken at the Amount of the Rent for One
Year, and of fuch further Sum in refpect of
the Fines from the faid Lands, as will amount
to a Sum equal to the Receipts of One Year,
on fuch Average as fhall be fettled or confirmed by the refpective Commiffioners before
whom the Queftion fhall be depending.

DEDUCTIONS.

As in the Firft Cafe, if payable by the
Owner.

FIFTH CASE.

*Lands demifed to Tenants in Confideration of a
Fine without Rent referved, or a nominal
Rent only.*

A fair Average of the Fines, as under
the Fourth Cafe.

DEDUCTIONS.

As under the Firft Cafe, if payable by the
Owner.

SIXTH

SIXTH CASE.

Houfes demifed to Tenants at Rack Rent.

The Annual Value of fuch Houfes fhall be taken at the full Amount of the Rent referved for One Year.

DEDUCTIONS.

Repairs, if not paid by the Tenant, as under the Second Cafe.

Other Deductions, as under the Firft Cafe, as far as the fame are applicable, if payable by the Owner.

SEVENTH CASE.

Houfes demifed to Tenants in Confideration of Rent referved and Fine.

As under the Fourth Cafe, *mutatis mutandis.*

DEDUCTIONS.

Repairs, if not paid by the Tenant, as under the Second Cafe.

Other Deductions, as under the Firft Cafe, as far as the fame are applicable, if payabie by the Owner.

I 3　　　EIGHTH

EIGHTH CASE.

*Houses demised to Tenants in Consideration of a
Fine, without Rent, or a nominal Rent only.*

As under the Fifth Case, *mutatis mutandis.*

DEDUCTIONS.

Repairs, if not paid by the Tenant, as
under the Second Case.

Other Deductions, as under the First
Case, as far as the same are applicable, if
payable by the Owner.

NINTH CASE.

Tythes in respect of Owners.

To be estimated on a fair Average for
Three Years preceding, of the actual Value,
if taken in Kind, Regard, in such Case, being had to the Expence incurred in collecting the same, or, if compounded for, of the
Compositions received for the same.

DEDUCTIONS.

As under the First Case, as far as the
same are applicable, if payable by the
Owner; and also all Payments made on Account of Parochial and other Rates, Taxes,
and Assessments, in respect of such Tythes
which shall be payable by the Owner.

TENTH

TENTH CASE.

Profits of Manors, or of Timber or Woods, ufually cut, periodically, and in certain Proportions, Mines, and other Profits of uncertain Annual Amount.

Value on fuch Average as fhall be fettled by the refpective Commiffioners, before whom the Queftion fhall be depending, except in the Cafe of Mines, where the Average fhall be taken on a Term not exceeding Five Years.

DEDUCTIONS.

As under the Firft Cafe, as far as the fame are applicable, if payable by the Owner.

2d. *INCOME of Tenants of Lands, Tenements, and Hereditaments.*

ELEVENTH CASE.

Lands or Hereditaments occupied by Tenants at Rack Rents.

If the Annual Value of fuch Lands or Hereditaments, eftimated as herein-before directed in the General Rule for eftimating the Annual Value of all Land, be under Three hundred Pounds, then the Income fhall be taken at not lefs than One Half, or more than Two Thirds of fuch Value; and

I 4 if

if at Three hundred Pounds or upwards, then at not lefs than Three Fifths or more than Three Fourths of fuch Value.

DEDUCTIONS.

Such and no other Dedu&ions as are herein-after comprized under the Head of GENERAL DEDUCTIONS, if payable by the Tenant.

TWELFTH CASE.

Mines, Tythes, Woods, and other Here-ditaments of uncertain Amount, when occu-pied by Tenants, to be charged as the fame would be charged in the Hands of the Owner, dedu&ing alfo the Rent payable for the fame.

THIRTEENTH CASE.

Lands or Tenements demifed in Confideration of Fines, whether with or without a Rent referved.

The Value of fuch Lands or Tenements fhall be eftimated at the Value at which the fame would be eftimated in the Cafe of an Owner occupying the fame, dedu&ing there-from a Sum equal to the Annual Value of Payments referved to the Owner, as dire&ed to be eftimated in the Fourth Cafe.

DEDUCTIONS as in the Eleventh Cafe.

3d. *INCOME*

3d. *INCOME of Mesne Lessors, under Demises, in Consideration of Fines, whether with or without a Rent reserved, and of Lands or Tenements demised upon improveable Leases.*

FOURTEENTH CASE.

In every such Case, every Mesne Lessor or Lessors shall be charged as Owner, deducting therefrom such Rent and Average of Fines (if any) as shall be paid thereout to his or her immediate Lessor.

II. *INCOME arising from Personal Property and from Trades, Professions, Offices, Pensions, Stipends, Employments, and Vocations.*

FIFTEENTH CASE.

1st. *INCOME from any Trade, Profession, Office, Pension, Stipend, Employment, or Vocation.*

The Annual Value to be taken for the First Year of being charged, either at not less than the full Amount of the Profits or Gains of such Trade, Profession, Office, Pension, Stipend, Employment, or Vocation, within

within the preceding Year, or, at the Elec-
tion of the Perſon charged, at a Sum not
leſs than the fair and juſt Average for One
Year of the Amount of the Profits or Gains
of ſuch Trade, Profeſſion, Office, Penſion,
Stipend, Employment, or Vocation, in the
Three Years preceding; and in all ſucceeding
Years, the Annual Value to be reckoned ac-
cording to the ſame Mode which the ſaid
Perſon ſhall have choſen to take in the Firſt
Year.

DEDUCTIONS.

No other Deductions to be made from ſuch
Annual Value, than ſuch as are herein-after
comprized under the Head of GENERAL DE-
DUCTIONS; except Two Thirds of the Rent
paid by the Tenants of Houſes, Part whereof
is occupied and uſed by ſuch Tenants as an
Open Shop for Retail Trade only; or by
Innkeepers and other Perſons licenſed to ſell
Wine, Ale, or other Liquors, by Retail; or
by Perſons keeping any School, Academy,
or Seminary for Learning, and uſually having their Scholars to board and lodge (to a
Number not leſs than Ten) in their reſpective
Dwelling Houſes; and alſo, except any Rate
charged in reſpect thereof by virtue of any
Act for granting an Aid to His Majeſty by
a Land Tax; or on Offices, Penſions, Sti-
pends, or Perſonal Eſtates, by any Act for
the Services of the Year for which the Computation ſhall be made; or upon Penſions,
or Salaries, Fees, and Wages, in reſpect of
Offices of Profit, by an Act, paſſed in the
Seventh

Seventh Year of the Reign of King *George* the Firſt; or upon Penſions, Gratuities, Offices, or Employments of Profit, by an Act, paſſed in the Thirty-firſt Year of His late Majeſty King *George* the Second,

SIXTEENTH CASE.

2d. INCOME *from Annuities, Intereſt of Money, Rent Charge, or other Payments of the like Nature.*

The Annual Value, with reſpect to Income derived from Property poſſeſſed by the ſame Perſon during the Whole of the preceding Year, to be taken at not leſs than the whole Income which became payable in reſpect thereof, within the Year preceding, ending on the Fifth Day of *February* in each Year, or on ſuch other Day of the Year as the Annual Payments have been uſually completed; and with reſpect to Income ariſing from Property not poſſeſſed by the ſame Perſon during the Whole of the preceding Year, at not leſs than the Whole Income (as far as the ſame can be computed) which will become payable in the ſucceeding Year.

GENERAL DEDUCTIONS to be allowed; and alſo any Tax or Charge in reſpect of the ſame, impoſed by any Act or Acts.

III. *INCOME*

III. *INCOME arising out of* Great Britain.

SEVENTEENTH CASE.

1st. *From Foreign Possessions.*

The full Amount of the actual Annual Net Income received in *Great Britain*, either estimating such Receipt in the First Year of being charged, at the Election of the Person charged, according to the Year ending the Fifth Day of *February* immediately preceding such Estimate, or according to the Average of the Three Years preceding such Fifth Day of *February*, or on such Day in each Year on which the Account of such Income has been usually made up; and in all succeeding Years, the Annual Receipt to be reckoned in the same Mode which the Person charged shall have chosen to take in the First Year.

GENERAL DEDUCTIONS to be allowed.

EIGHTEENTH CASE.

2d. *MONEY arising from Foreign Securities.*

The Annual Income of such Securities, if the same were existing in the preceding Year,
to

to be eftimated according to the Produce of fuch Year, and if the fame were not then exifting, to be computed upon the expected Produce of the current Year.

GENERAL DEDUCTIONS to be allowed.

IV. *INCOME not falling under any of the foregoing Rules.*

Such Income to be eftimated to the beft of the Knowledge and Belief of the Perfon entitled thereto; and fuch Eftimate to be delivered to the Commiffioners, together with a Statement of the Nature of fuch Income, and the Grounds on which the Amount thereof fhall have been fo eftimated.

GENERAL DEDUCTIONS to be allowed.

GENERAL DEDUCTIONS FROM INCOME.

1. The Amount of Annual Intereft payable for Debts owing by the Party, or charged upon the Property of the Party, from which any Income fhall arife.

2. The Amount of Allowances to any Child or Children, or other Relations, fuch Child or Children, or other Relation or Relations,

lations, not making a Part of the Family of the Party, and of whose Names and Places of Residence the Assessors and Surveyors shall have had Notice.

3. Assessed Taxes under the Two Acts of the Thirty-eighth Year of the Reign of His present Majesty, for repealing the Duties on Houses, Windows, and Lights, on Inhabited Houses, and on Clocks and Watches; and for granting to His Majesty other Duties on Houses, Windows, and Lights, and on Inhabited Houses, in lieu thereof: And for repealing the Duties upon Male Servants, Carriages, Horses, Mules, and Dogs, and for granting to His Majesty other Duties in lieu thereof.

4. The Amount of any Annuity payable by the Party, either as a Debt or Charge upon his or her Income, (excepting any Payment to the Wife of any Party living with such Party, for which she, or any Trustee or Trustees on her Behalf, shall not be duly charged under this Act.)

5. Persons who have made or shall make Insurance on their respective Lives, or on the Lives of their respective Wives, shall be at Liberty, in Addition to any other Deductions, to deduct the Amount of the Premium of such Insurance for the current Year.

6. Persons entitled to any Income during and depending upon the Life or Lives of any other Person or Persons who have made, or shall make Insurance on the Life or Lives of such other Person or Persons, shall be at Liberty,

c. 40, 41.

Liberty, in Addition to any other Deductions, (except the Deduction herein-after mentioned), to deduct the Amount of the Premiums of such last mentioned Insurance for the current Year; provided that if, after the Death of such other Person or Persons on whose Life or Lives such Insurance shall have been made, the Income, or any Part thereof from which such Premiums have been deducted, shall be continued, or the Estate from whence the same arose renewed, or shall have been usually continued, or the Estate from whence the same arose shall have been usually renewed by the Payment of a Fine or Fines, then and in such Case no Deduction shall be allowed on Account of such Fine or Fines which shall have been paid, or would become payable, on any such Renewal.

PARTICULAR DEDUCTIONS FROM INCOME.

1. The Amount of the Tenths paid by any Ecclesiastical Person within the Year preceding that in which the Computation shall be made.

2. Procurations and Synodals paid by Ecclesiastical Persons, on an Average of Seven Years preceding that in which the Computation shall be made.

3. Repairs of Chancels of Churches by any Rector, Vicar, or other Person bound to repair the same, on an Average of Twenty-one Years preceding, as aforesaid.

(B.)

STATEMENTS of INCOME.

In the Cafes of all Perfons refident in Great Britain, and Perfons generally refident out of Great Britain, having Income under Two hundred Pounds:

I *A. B.* do declare, That my Income [*or, in the Cafe of a Truftee, Agent, Receiver, Guardian, Tutor, Curator, or Committee,* that the Income of *C. D. or,* of the Corporation, Company, Fraternity, or Society of   as the Cafe may be, for whom I am a Truftee, Agent, Receiver, Guardian, Tutor, Curator, or Committee] eftimated according to the Directions and Rules of an Act, paffed in the Thirtyninth Year of the Reign of His prefent Majefty, intituled, *An Act* [*here fet forth the Title of the Act*] doth not exceed the Sum of   [*in all Cafes where the Income exceeds Sixty Pounds, and does not amount to Two hundred Pounds, add alfo*] and that I am willing to pay the Sum of   for my Contribution [*or, in the Cafe of a Truftee, Agent, Receiver, Guardian, Tutor, Curator, or Committee,* I do propofe on Behalf of the
                                        faid

said *C. D.* that the Sum of
should be paid for his, [her, *or* their] Con-
tribution] for One Year, from the Fifth Day
of *April* to the Fifth Day of *April*
the same being not less than One
Part of my [*or*, his, her, *or* their]
Income, estimated as aforesaid, to be paid
according to the Directions of the said Act.
Dated the

Signed

WE whose Names are underwritten do
testify that the Signature of is of
his proper Hand Writing, and that the same
was signed in our Presence.

INCOME *of* TWO HUNDRED POUNDS, *or upwards:*

I *A. B.* do declare, That I am willing to
pay the Sum of for my Con-
tribution [*or, in the Case of a Trustee, Agent,
Receiver, Guardian, Tutor, Curator, or Committee, or in the Case of any Corporation,
Company, Fraternity, or Society of Persons,* I
A. B. do propose on the Behalf of *C. D.* or
of the Corporation, Company, Fraternity, or
Society of [*as the Case may be*]
for whom I am Trustee, Agent, Receiver,
Guardian, Tutor, Curator, or Committee,
that the Sum of should be paid
for his, [her *or* their] Contribution] for One
Year, from the Fifth Day of *April*

K until

until the Fifth Day of *April*

in purfuance of an Act, intituled, *An Act*, &c.   And I do declare, That the faid Sum of   is not lefs than One Tenth Part of my [*or*, his, her, *or* their] Income, eftimated according to the Directions and Rules prefcribed by the faid Act, to the beft of my Knowledge and Belief. Dated

Signed

WE whofe Names are underwritten do teftify that the Signature of is of his proper Hand Writing, and that the fame was figned in our Prefence.

NOTICE

(C.)

NOTICE to be given to the Assessors by any Person engaged in Trade or Manufacture, or by any Body, Corporation, Company, Fraternity, or Society.

TAKE Notice, That I, [*or* We, *if Partners, or if not on his own Account,* on the Behalf of] am [*or* are] engaged in Trade or Manufacture, viz. [*Here set forth the Branch or Branches of Trade or Manufacture, and the Place or Places where the same is carried on*] and mean to be charged to the Rates and Duties granted by an Act of the Thirty-ninth Year of the Reign of His present Majesty, under the Powers and Provisions vested in and given to the Commercial Commissioners for the of in the County of

SCHEDULE

(D.)

SCHEDULE of INCOME of

No.	DESCRIPTION of PROPERTY from which INCOME arises.	Annual Value.		
		£.	s.	d.
1.	Lands occupied by me as Owner			
2.	Houses and Buildings occupied by me as Owner			
3.	Lands in Occupation of Tenants at Rack Rent			
4.	Lands demised to Tenants in consideration of a Fine paid and Rent reserved { Amount of Fines, on an Average of Years — Amount of Rent —			
5.	Lands demised to Tenants in consideration of a Fine, without any Rent reserved, or nominal Rent only { Amount of Fines received, upon an Average of Years —			
6.	Houses demised to Tenants at Rack Rent			
7.	Houses demised to Tenants in consideration of Rent reserved and Fine			
8.	Houses demised to Tenants in consideration of a Fine without Rent, or a nominal Rent only			
9.	Tythes received in Kind, or Composition reserved for the same { Amount of Average Receipt for Three Years —			
10.	Profits of { Manors — Average Receipt for Years; Timber — D° — D°; Woods — D° — D°; Mines — D° not exceeding Five Years; Other Profits of uncertain Amount — D° for Years			
11.	Lands or Hereditaments demised to me, as Tenant at Rack Rent			
	Carry over —			

(D.)

A. B. [*Description*] of the Division of

DEDUCTIONS.	£.	s.	d.		£.	s.	d.
Land Tax payable on the several Properties mentioned under N^os on the other Side, from the 　Day of　 to the 　Day of　 last past –				For One Year preceding the Delivery of this Schedule.			
Fines paid upon an Average of 　Years –							
Fee Farm Rents payable out of N^os on the other Side 　–　　–　　–							
Quit Rents, payable out of N^os 　D^o –							
Rent Charges, payable out of N^os 　D^o –							
Ground Rent, payable out of N^os 　D^o –							
Other Rents, payable out of N^os 　D^o –							
Tenths 　–　　–　　–							
Procurations, Synodals, payable (by Ecclefiaſtical Perſons) out of N^o upon an Average of Seven Years 　–　　–							
Repairs {Of Farm, with principal Meſſuage, under N^os 　–　　–　　–							
Of Farm Buildings, without principal Meſſuage, under N^os 　–　　–　　–							
Of draining Lands, under N^os 　–　　–							
Of Embankments, under N^os 　–　　–							
Of Houſes and Buildings not occupied with a Farm, under N^os 　–　　–							
Of Chancels of Churches by Rectors, Vicars, and others bound to repair the same, upon an Average of 21 Years 　–　　–　　–							
Carry over　–　　–							

No.	DESCRIPTION of PROPERTY from which INCOME arises.	Annual Value

Brought over — —

No.	Description	£. s. d.	£. s. d.
12.	**Profits of** { Manors — — } demised to me,— Timber — — *Average the same* Woods — — *as the 10th Case,* Other Hereditaments { *deducting the* of uncertain Amount } *Rent payable.* Tythes { taken in Kind } { as in the 9th Case, { compounded for } { deducting the Rent.		
13.	Lands or Tenements demised to me in consideration of a Fine, whether with or without a Rent reserved; Annual Value — — — — — —		
14.	Lands or Tenements demised to me in consideration of Fine, with or without a Rent, and underlet to a Tenant — — Lands demised to me at Rent, and underlet to a Tenant, at an improved Rent —	£. s. d.	
15.	From Profession, Offices, Pensions, Stipends, Employment, Trade, or Vocation — — — — —		
16.	From Annuities, Interest of Money, Rent Charge, and other Payments and Allowances applied to my Use, including Income of the Wife, if any, for which she or her Trustee or Trustees shall not be charged by virtue of this Act, living with Husband, though separately secured — — — — — — —		
17.	From Foreign Possessions — — — —		
18.	From Money arising from Foreign Securities — —		
19.	From any Income not falling under any of the above Heads, or within the Rules prescribed by the Act — Nature of the Income, and Grounds on which the Amount thereof is estimated — — —		

Total Amount of Property — £.

Deductions from above — —

Income chargeable — —£.

DEDUCTIONS.

	£. s. d.	£. s. d.
Brought over — —		

Tythes {
Expences in collecting the same, upon an Average of Three Years — —
Value thereof paid in Kind, upon Dᵒ Average
Value of Composition for the same, upon Dᵒ Average — — — — —
}

	£. s. d.	

Annual Interest payable { Personal — —
for Debts — — { Charged on Nᵒˢ —

Allowances to Children, or other Relations; viz. [   ]

Assessed Taxes under Acts 38 Geo. III. c. 40. & 41. — —

Annuities — — — — — — —

Land Tax on Personal Estates, Offices, Pensions, &c. — —

Premiums of Insurance on Life — — — — —

Total Amount of Deductions — — —£.

Memorandum :—*The local Situation of the several Properties in the opposite Column must here be described under their respective Numbers; and if in Great Britain, the several Parishes and Counties in which they are situate, together with the several Places of Residence of the Party.*

Witness my Hand, this   Day of

(E.)

ECLARATION of the Number of CHILDREN.

A. B. do declare, That I have the under-mentioned
ld (*or* Children) born in lawful Wedlock, and main-
ed by me at my Expence; (*videlicet,*) *C. D.* of the
: of   *E. F.* of the Age of   and
H. of the Age of   .   in respect of whom I
m an Abatement in pursuance of the said Act, and am
ly to verify this my Declaration as the Act requires.

(F.)

PRECEPT of the COMMISSIONERS.

VE   being   of the Commissioners appointed
:arry into Execution the general Purposes of an Act,
ed in the Thirty-ninth Year of the Reign of His present
esty, intituled, *An Act,* [*here set forth the Title of the*
] for the   of   do hereby require you to re-
, or cause to be returned, within the Space of Ten Days
r the Date of this our Precept, at our Office, situate at
        between the Hour of   .   in the Forenoon
the Hour of   in the Afternoon, unto us, or
of the Commissioners appointed for the Purposes afore-
, for the said   of   who shall be there pre-
at the Time of making your Return, a Schedule of.
iculars of Property from which your Income, charge-
under the said Act, ought to be estimated, with the
ount of Deductions to be made therefrom, under the
ds contained in, and according to the Forms hereunto
:xed, or such of them as the Case shall require.
reof fail not.

Given under our Hands, this   Day of

F I N I S.

CPSIA information can be obtained
at www.ICGtesting.com
Printed in the USA
BVHW052252060223
657976BV00027B/321